Dr. John Coleman

BEYOND THE CONSPIRACY
Unmasking the invisible
WORLD GOVERNMENT

ⵔMNIA VERITAS.

John Coleman

John Coleman is a British author and former member of the Secret Intelligence Service. Coleman has produced various analyses of the Club of Rome, the Giorgio Cini Foundation, Forbes Global 2000, the Interreligious Peace Colloquium, the Tavistock Institute, the Black Nobility and other organisations with New World Order themes.

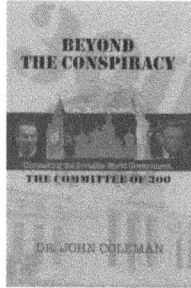

BEYOND THE CONSPIRACY
Unmasking the invisible world government

© Omnia Veritas Ltd – 2023

⊘MNIA VERITAS.

www.omnia-veritas.com

The English author and MI6 operative H.G. Wells in his work *The Open Conspiracy* wrote about the lack of understanding of "the common man" of secret societies, as did Dr. Jacob Mass, the biographer for Justice Brandeis, who said that secret deals are made about which it is very difficult to obtain definitive information, until they are lost in the antiquities of time when men are apt to write their memoirs. It has been commented on many times during the course of history that the average person in most countries has little or no time to spare to think beyond making a living, raising a family and holding down a job to make these objectives possible. This leaves little or no time to attend to politics or matters of economics or other vital issues, such as war and peace that affect their lives and the life of the nation.

Governments know this. So it seems, do highly organized groups operating behind many different front organizations which always have the edge over the citizenry. What the average individual does not know—and will probably never know—is that all great historical events are planned in secret by men in total privacy. Dr. Gerard Encausse in his work *Mysteria* of April 14, 1914 put it this way:

> *Side by side with the international politics of each State, there exists certain obscure organizations. The men who take part in these councils are not professional politicians or brilliantly dressed ambassadors, but certain unknown men, high financiers, who are superior to the vain ephemeral politicians who imagine that they govern the world.*

Such a group were the men of the English East India Company, whose antecedents sprang from the Catharis, the Bogomils and the Albigensians who had originated from Manichean Babylon, and who went on to become the controllers of not only England, but of the whole world. It has been the experience throughout recorded history that one of the common denominator is man's desire to control. No matter what societal structure is examined, there is always a group of certain individuals, in whom the need to control is paramount, and who form themselves into secret societies. Anyone who seeks to expose these societies places himself in danger.

This is one of the reasons why the Committee of 300 has been so successful in concealing its existence from the broad mass of the American people, so much so that they are now not afraid to move beyond the conspiracy into the open. Apparently, a small number of researchers felt that there had to be some kind of an upper-echelon coordinating, controlling body, that oversees and coordinates the activities of the "local level" agencies, of which the Federal Reserve Banks is but one of many. They were generally lumped together under the title, "secret societies." The purpose of this book is to go beyond the conspiracy and open the doors to these secret societies to how mankind is really governed and by whom.

My thanks to the many friends and supporters of my work who have helped me so much to weather the attacks on my work and who have been generous in their financial support in times of financial duress; thereby making it possible for this book to be published in the face of stringent opposition.

This book is an account of the master plan of the One World Government that was disclosed to participants of the misnamed Interreligious Peace Colloquim held at Bellago, Italy in 1972. The misnamed master peace plan was put into action in Yugoslavia for the first time in order to destroy it as a nation state. Therefore, the greater part of this book is about what happened there, because it was a "role model" for future actions.

Iraq may well be the last country to be invaded by a One World Government military force. Based upon what was learned from the conquest of Yugoslavia, the opinion of conspiracy watchers is that the plan that toppled Milosevic is the way future recalcitrant governments will be brought to heel. Thus, a detailed study of the methodology and strategic employed to destroy Yugoslavia completed in recent years is of the utmost importance.

Dr. John Coleman, September 2007

FOREWORD

It is to be hoped that you, the reader, will already be familiar with my book *"The Conspirator's Hierarchy: The Story of the Committee of 300,"* which was published in its Fourth Edition in January 2007. It may otherwise be difficult to envisage the scope of this book. The truth is that very few of the public has adequate means to make sense out of events that seem beyond reality are brought to our limited experience and knowledge so we mistakenly think—it cannot be so. With such a background, the average person cannot view with certainty the massive changes, nearly always for the worse that are happening in other areas of the nation and the world, as a conspiracy, let alone even begin to understand that they are part of a deliberately engineered plan to bring about dislocations. These deliberately engineered dislocations are not perceived as such, because the majorities do not think in that way. The end of the continuity of family life, the loss of a job that has been "in the family" for many generations (in an auto plant for example); a forced move from the neighborhood we love, leaving behind friends, the church, and all the familiar and comfortable things. The average person never ascribes these upheavals and distortions of their lives to more than happenstance. They simply do not know any better, and cannot conceive that what has befallen them is something far different from mere happenstance.

The noted English author and MI6 operative H.G. Wells in his work *The Open Conspiracy,* wrote about the lack of understanding of "the common man" of secret societies, as did Dr. Jacob Hass, the biographer for the American Justice

Brandeis, who said that secret deals are made about, which it is very difficult to obtain definitive information, until they are lost in the antiquities of time when men are apt to write their memoirs. It has been commented upon many times during the course of history that the average person in most countries has little or no time to spare to think beyond making a living, raising a family and holding down a job to make these objectives possible. This leaves little or no time to attend to politics, matters of economics or other vital issues, such as war and peace that affect their lives and the life of the nation. Governments know this. So it seems do highly organized groups operating behind many different front organizations, which always have the edge over the local citizenry. What the average individual does not know—and will probably never know—is that all great historical events are planned in secret by men in total privacy. Dr. Gerard Encausse in his work *Mysteria* of April 14, 1914 put it this way:

> *Side by side with the international politics of each State; there exists certain obscure organizations... The men who take part in these councils are not professional politicians or brilliantly dressed ambassadors, but certain unknown men, high financiers who are superior to the vain ephemeral politicians who imagine that they govern the world.*

Such a group were the men of the British East India Company, whose antecedents sprang from the Catharis, the Bogomils and the Albigensians who had originated from Manichean Babylon and who went on to become the controllers of not only England, but of the whole world.

It has been the experience throughout recorded history that one of the common denominators is man's desire to control. No matter the societal structure; there has always been a group of certain individuals in whom the need to control is paramount and who form themselves into secret societies. Anyone who seeks to expose these societies puts himself in danger.

This is one of the reasons why the Committee of 300 has been so successful in concealing its existence from the broad mass of the American people, so much so that they are now willing to move beyond the conspiracy into the open. Apparently, a small number of researchers felt that there had to be some kind of an upper-echelon coordinating, controlling body, that oversees and coordinates the activities of the "local level" agencies of which the Federal Reserve Banks is but one of many. They were generally lumped together under the title, "secret societies." The purpose of this book is to go beyond the conspiracy and open the doors to how mankind is really governed and by whom.

Chapter 1

The Rise of Pantheist Deistic Unitarians

Almost three hundred years later the most important of these families was the Rockefellers who owned and controlled the Rockefeller-Standard Oil dynasty. It was this network that was used by the "300" to usher in the Fabian Socialist "New Deal" via Roosevelt and dispossess the American people of their gold. Most of these families, while outwardly professing Christianity were pantheist, Gnostic, Rosicrucian and deistic Unitarians. Their philosophy was very markedly Socialist.

This is best understood when we consider that the ancestors of some of these families could be traced back to the Anabaptists and Wycliff s Lollards, whose politics were distinctly Communist, although Communism as an established doctrine did not yet exist. There exists a school of thought that there may have been elements of the Bogomils among them who had fled to the New World from the Balkans during the Inquisition and also a number of descendants of the Khazars, a barbaric race of Indo-Turk origin, that lived along the lower reaches of the Volga in Russia, until they were driven out by the Princes of Moscow led by Prince Dimitri Donskoi. (*Encyclopedia Britannica*, 1915)

The Rockefeller family and the Astor family are believed to have emigrated to the U.S. from Asia Minor with this mixture of races and alien cultures dating back to the Manicheans. (*Rockefeller Internationalist*, Emmanuel Josephson 1952)

The East India Company, with its charter granted by the monarchy and its successor, the British East India Company men, had a habit of giving grants to Christian evangelicals. Rockefeller and his fellow-travelers followed suit, fostering evangelical Christianity to hide their true intentions, which was to attain political power in the United States and then around the world as old John D. demonstrated.

In the United States it was the Christian Fundamentalist introduced by the British East India Companies, John Nelson Darby as "Dispensationalism" favored by the China Inland Mission and in South Africa prior to the Anglo Boer War, by the London Missionary Society, which gave rise to the war in 1899 by its meddlesome political interference. All of these Christian organizations appear to have been well funded. The Quakers established Communist-like communes during the Revolutionary War and enjoyed strong financial support from William Aldrich (an ancestor of Nelson Aldrich Rockefeller).

The Rothschild family was the leading conspirators working to install a Central Bank in the U.S. in flagrant violation of the U.S. Constitution forbidding such an institution. What we saw with the installation of the Federal Reserve Bank was the consolidation of the grip of the Committee of 300 on America.

It followed the American foreign policy and the wars that America has fought over the course of the nineteenth century (including the Spanish American War in 1898 and the present so-called War on Terror) have successfully extended the cartel's control over the world economy. Without the successful establishment of a Central Bank in the United States, all wars that were fought after 1912 would have been impossible to finance. The American Civil War was fought to determine control of the U.S. economy. The issue of slavery was of little import; the North cared little about slavery. Many of the Union Army generals were slave owners, as was Mrs. Lincoln, the wife of Abraham Lincoln. The Civil War, like all wars, was fought over economic issues. Slavery was a mere red herring and was not the basic cause of the war. Americans being easily misled through their trust in Government did not know the true cause of the tragic war.

Again, let me make it clear: All wars are economic wars in their origin and purpose. The South had a perfect right to secede if its citizens so desired, because of the economic issues between the North and the South. The implication is that America has accumulated its "only superpower" international position by some accident and not by design. Arguments for a contrary view elicit derisive accusations of falling victim to "conspiracy theory."

Reassuringly, Americans believe that self-interested individuals and organizations are incapable of collaboration in a conspiracy to achieve common causes. When J.P. Morgan sat the owners of America's railroads around a table and hammered out a non-competing agreement, it was no accident. *In fact it was a conspiracy.* None of America's wars were accidents and have been far more profitable than will ever be made public. The U.S. confiscated billions of dollars worth of German and Japanese war treasure at the end of World War II. President Truman made a conscious decision to not reveal this to the public and not repatriate it at the close of hostilities. Instead, it was; and is still being used to finance covert operations.

The widespread belief that the much-hated trusts were broken up in the first decade of the twentieth century due to crusading by Theodore Roosevelt was certainly without foundation. Roosevelt no doubt used his public stance against "big business" to successfully bid for campaign money from the very businessmen whom he was attacking. This perhaps explains why he subsequently signed legislation repealing criminal penalties for those same businessmen. This is a common thread that runs through "liberal," conservative or "progressive" U.S. Presidents. Franklin D. Roosevelt wished to be remembered as the champion of the downtrodden, who ended the Great Depression. He established the nation's social security system, which in reality is funded by a highly regressive tax on its beneficiaries. Matching contributions from business were allowed to be deducted as a business expense before tax, which simply extended the regressive nature of the program by financing business' share out of foregone tax revenue. Roosevelt, a superb politician, won a landslide victory on a platform of reform, which he never had the slightest intention of carrying out.

In fact, he did the opposite by declaring a national economic emergency, short-circuiting any constitutional challenge to his power in the court. He promptly defaulted on the gold clause in the government's bond contracts and established the Exchange Stabilization Fund (ESF) in 1934; ostensibly meant to promote dollar stability in the foreign exchanges markets it is exempt from reporting to Congress and is answerable only to the President and Secretary of the Treasury. It is, in short, an undisclosed fund that can tap Federal Government credit, an unconstitutional and very dangerous practice.

Establishment of the ESF was merely an extension of the same logic behind the creation of the Federal Reserve in 1914. The latter, the Federal Reserve was also created in response to a crisis: the crash of 1907. Wall Street legend credits J.P. Morgan's genius and patriotism with saving the Nation. In reality, the crash and resulting depression enabled Morgan to destroy his competitors, buy up their assets and in the process revealing to the nation and the world just how powerful the Wall Street and international banks and Morgan were.

Not all were grateful and some demanded legislative action to bring the federal credit and national monetary system under public oversight and control. In a campaign of masterful political legerdemain, the Federal Reserve was created in 1912 by an act of Congress to do just that. But by creating it as a private corporation owned by the banks, Congress effectively ceded to the banks a position even stronger than they had occupied before. Even today it is not widely understood that the Federal Reserve is a privately held business owned by the very interests that it nominally regulates.

Thus the control of federal credit and the U.S. monetary system and the rich flow of insider information that results from that control are veiled from public view and are privately controlled in secret which rather explains the Sphinx-like nature of the Federal Reserve chairman. It is not generally understood that every single one of these agencies were set up in open defiance of the U.S. Constitution, thereby boldly signaling that the conspiracy need no longer be kept dark. Only one man in the Congress recognized the Federal Reserve as an unconstitutional therefore, illegal entity.

Congressman Louis T. McFadden was that man. He filed suit against the Federal Reserve claiming it had stolen billions of dollars from the American people, and demanded the return of the money. But McFadden was murdered before his lawsuit came before a court and thus nothing came of it. Another unconstitutional action on a par with the Federal Reserve was the CIA Act of 1949, which created a budget mechanism that allowed the CIA to spend as much money as it wanted "without regard to the provisions of law and regulations relating to the expenditure of government funds." In short, the CIA has a way to fund anything—legal or illegal—behind the barrier of national security laws and Congress has stood by and allowed this unconstitutional organization to usurp its authority without lifting a finger to stop such a deplorable violation of the U.S. Constitution and loss of its powers.

Chapter 2

The Narcotics Trade

It may seem strange to the majority of readers to think there could be a positive connection between narcotics trafficking and the stock market, but consider: in the late 1990s the U.S. Department of Justice estimated that the proceeds of such trade entering the U.S. banking system were between $500 and $1000 billion annually, or more than 5–10% of Gross Domestic Product (GDP). The proceeds of crime need to find a way into legitimate, that is legal channels or they are worthless to the holders. If one further imagines that the banking system earns a fee of 1% for handling, then the profits for the banks from narcotic activity is in the region of $5 to $10 billion.

Applying Citigroup's current stock market multiple of 15 or so to this yields a market capitalization of anywhere from $65 to $115 billion. One can thus readily see the importance of the illegal drug trade to the financial services industry. As it happens, this trade in illegal profits is concentrated in four states: Texas, New York, Florida and California, or four Federal Reserve districts: Dallas, New York, Atlanta and San Francisco. Can anyone seriously suppose that the Federal Reserve is unaware of this even if the Department of Justice is? It, after all, handles the flow and must know where it comes from.

One reason for the Federal Reserve's silence is that agencies of the government itself have been involved in drug trafficking for sixty years or more, as I detail in my work, *The Drug Trade from A to* Z. For the purposes of understanding the black budget used by the CIA and others, one needs to be aware of the American practice of opening the American consumer market for drugs to foreign exporters in order to pursue strategic objectives abroad. The portability of narcotics and the huge price mark up from production to point of sale makes them a particularly useful source of financing for covert operations. Even more important is that the proceeds from narcotics sales fall completely outside conventional, constitutional channels of funding. This helps explain narcotics trafficking in zones of conflict around the world, from Columbia to Afghanistan. For example, since hostilities began in Afghanistan with NATO forces involved, opium poppy cultivation and production of raw opium has burgeoned from 3000 to 6000 tons a year.

Little examined, however, is the impact of narcotics trafficking on communities and economies at the point of sale. Consider, for example, the impact on real estate markets and financial services. Real estate is an attractive area in which to employ the cash surplus resulting from narcotics sales because it is, as an industry, entirely unregulated with respect to money laundering. Because cash is an acceptable and in some places familiar method of payment, large sums can be disposed of easily and with little comment. This can and does result in considerable distortion to local demand, and in turn provides fuel for real estate speculation and increased credit demand to finance it along with considerable opportunities for speculation and fraud.

The Iran Contra imbroglio during the 1980s contained all these elements; although many are familiar with the sale of arms to Iran to provide cash to finance CIA backed guerrillas in Nicaragua and death squads in El Salvador, it is less well-known less to them, that local financial institutions and narcotics sales in the U.S. banking allows the application of leverage to the cash that is generated by "illegal" activity, while simultaneously making it possible to launder the funds. And when a bank fails, it is the shareholders, uninsured depositors and the taxpayers who pick up the bill. The point here is narcotics trafficking creates a milieu in which the incentives to engage in uneconomic activity are greater than those to engage in economic activity. In a word, the profits from stealing are higher than the profits from playing by the rules.

The government's power combined with advancing computer technology has over the last forty years made the managing of national—and by extension the international—cash flow easy.

American victory in the Second World War meant that the entire West and its dependencies were co-opted into the International Monetary Fund (IMF) negotiated at Bretton Woods in 1944. Forty-five years later, the collapse of the Soviet Union in 1989 meant that for the first time in history there was no alternative monetary or political choice in the international arena. The British Empire had surrendered to the Americans precisely because America represented an alternative to sterling, namely the dollar.

Today the U.S. presides over a more or less fully closed global monetary system based on the dollar. In practice this means that those countries within the system must exchange real value in the form of natural resources like oil and gas, manufactured items and commodities with the U.S. cartel in exchange for dollars, which are no more than an accounting entry created out of thin air. This is analogous to a company with no assets exchanging watered stock for cash, and indeed this is no accident. It was a favored technique by which the J.P. Morgan dynasty of the nineteenth century successfully financed the consolidation of American industry and finance.

Their heirs are busily doing the same thing, but on a global scale. And it is all out in the open, beyond the conspiracy stage. Because of its unique finance control, the U.S. has been able to embark on costly global military adventures the outcome of which is far from certain. This marks the culmination of more than fifty years of continuous overt and covert warfare. In this it is supported by the most sophisticated financing apparatus in history, capable of mobilizing the cash generated from a wide variety of activities both open and covert. The price has been the progressive hollowing out of the American economy itself, and the progressive erosion of civil liberties and the rule of law. It will also be the end of this Republic.

All Wars Begin with Contrived Situations

The War Party has usually managed to maintain control of American foreign policy through its virtually ironclad grip on the political process. This has been achieved by its mastery of the two-party system that has enshrined the Democrats and the Republicans as the only two real options for American voters. Even when the American people opposed interventionism—as in the run-up to World War II, for one example—the pro-war elites manipulated the political process and made sure that the voters were presented with two warmongering candidates instead of just one. In 1968, at the height of the Vietnam War, a carefully stage-managed delegate-selection process gypped Eugene McCarthy out of the Democratic presidential nomination. At the level of presidential politics, the system failed only once, in the case of George McGovern, and has worked since then with ruthless efficiency in making sure the people of the United States *never* get to vote on the direction of U.S. foreign policy.

This is how we get into wars, despite popular antiwar sentiment, and it is how we stay in them—regardless of the huge percentage of the American public who say our present occupation of Iraq is pointless. Yet there are signs the War Party's stranglehold over the leadership of at least one major party is beginning to fray. This unraveling is a response to the grassroots antiwar sentiment that is energizing a burgeoning number of Democratic Party activists—both old and new—forcing the moribund leadership to either come out against the occupation of Iraq or else join Senator Joe Lieberman, the President's most stalwart supporter when it comes to the war. Some say it is because Bush is such a sure backer of Israel. Indeed, Lieberman is more royalist than the king, attacking any idea of a drawdown in troops as impermissible, and even demanding an end to all discussion of withdrawal, and that the U.S. attack Iran.

This last is what the Lieberman wing of Democrats has always been about: limiting debate, shutting down discussion, and policing the party's candidates and organizational structure at the precinct level to ensure that no challenge to interventionism and militarism arises from the grassroots. They are the last of the Scoop Jackson Democrats, forerunners of today's "Neo-Conservatives," who were more warlike than many Republicans in the Cold War era, and always insisted that politics must stop at the water's edge, (i.e., foreign policy must never be debated) and the grand bipartisan consensus in favor of global intervention must be allowed to continue unchallenged, forever.

The Neo-Conservatives are usually thought of as being exclusively Republicans, but this ignores their history as a political and ideological tendency—and the background of the Scoop Jackson Democrats, notably Richard Perle, a Jackson aide; Elliot Abrams, former chief of staff to Senator Daniel P. Moynihan and such "Neo-Bolsheviks" notables as Ben Wattenberg, Joshua Muravchik and Marshall.

It was Truman, of course, who set the precedent of assuming the power to send troops overseas short of a war declaration—a feat not even Franklin Roosevelt, who openly aspired to be a dictator, dared attempt.

As the American Republic began to change into an empire, it was thought necessary—by the leaders of both parties—to give the chief executive imperial powers, i.e., the power to make war without consulting anyone. In 1950, when President Truman dispatched U.S. troops to Korea, only a few Republicans opposed his usurpation of the Constitution and warned that Americans would one day regret standing idly by and letting it happen.

"If the President can intervene in Korea without

congressional approval," said Senator Robert A. Taft" ... he can go to war in Malaysia or Indonesia or Iran or South America."

In any case, the Truman Democrats are having a hard time these days: the party's grassroots—and specifically the so-called "net-roots" — are having a real impact, for the first time since the Vietnam War. Lieberman's fervent support for the war has provoked opposition, and he faced a party primary, with millionaire Ned Lamont, who had made the war the major issue of the campaign, gaining steadily in the polls. Lamont was chosen as the party candidate over Lieberman who then petitioned to appear on the ballot as an "Independent."

Lieberman's support for the war was unpopular with the voters, but apparently very heavily financed and backed by the AIPAC Lobby; he defeated Lamont and was re-elected to another four years in the Senate. As the co-chairman of the revived Committee on the Present Danger, Lieberman serves as front man for the most radical wing of the Neo-Bolshevik movement: such preeminent warmongers as James R. "World War IV" Woolsey, Ken "Cakewalk" Adelman, Frank Gaffney and Midge Decter among many others who believe that U.S. support for Israel is the most important issue in American politics. But of course "the terrorists" (i.e., the Iraqi insurgents) can—and *are*—defeating us militarily.

They are victorious as long as they can maintain the present stalemate. As for the disappointment of the American people, when it comes to this war, it stems from being lied to; and being led into a quagmire. The recent conviction of "Scooter" Libby, chief of staff to Vice President Dick Cheney has opened a nasty—smelling can of muck of just how much and how widespread was the panoply of lies and deceit that took the U.S. into Iraq for the second time. Not that it will make any appreciable difference. The conspirators are embarked upon a course of action that is right out in the open, in short, the Bush administration and their British partners have now moved far beyond the conspiracy stage.

The idea that the neo-medievalism of Osama bin Laden & Co. represents as great a threat as Communism and/or Fascism is absurd on its face: the international Communist movement, at its height, represented millions of committed ideologues who were, in turn, backed up by the nuclear-armed Soviet Union and its satellites. In practically every country on Earth, the Kremlin's highly-disciplined agents agitated and recruited to their cause, rising in response to Moscow's call and keeping a low profile when discretion was the order of the day.

The Islamist revolutionaries, on the other hand, can claim no such advantages: they do not hold state power anywhere, and their following is largely confined to the Middle East and North Africa, with little outposts of support in Afghanistan and South Asia. Furthermore, this fantasy of "a new evil empire," in the form of a worldwide Islamist "caliphate" is not a very convincing bogeyman. Aside from the futility of uniting a largely dysfunctional Arab-Muslim community of nations, which would only achieve dysfunction on a much larger scale—this so-called "caliphate " would threaten no one in the West. Israel which, last time I looked at a map is not situated in the West—would be the only potential loser.

As for the comparison to fascism and National Socialism: Nazi Germany, at its height, commanded the mightiest war machine on Earth. Hitler was the master of Europe and his armies were marching on Moscow, encircling the remnants of resistance to German hegemony by seizing North Africa and preparing to move on the British.

Where is a comparable force anywhere in the Muslim world? Bush and Cheney are living out an episode of historical fiction, in which they are the heroic truth-tellers who dare to swim against the current of opinion within their own party. They do battle in the name of fighting for "democracy" against the latter— day "appeasers;" who, the implication is clear, are soft on the war because they are secretly (or not so secretly) sympathetic to the enemy.

According to Lieberman, if Democrats oppose this futile war launched on the basis of a lie, then the terrorists will have won because we will have allowed them to "divide us and defeat us politically." If you're antiwar, you're pro al-Qaeda. This is what Lieberman's message has been and he is just as consistent on this question as George W. Bush—if a bit more vehement about it.

The Bush-Cheney view that we are engaged in this epic battle— akin to the struggle against Hitlerism and Stalinism—is shared by exactly no one who knows anything about al Qaeda or the Middle East and has an ounce of common sense. Both Communism and Fascism were mass movements that seized power in several countries and were capable of waging a conventional military assault on the United States.

Those radical Islamists who have declared war on America are the numerically small vanguard of a worldwide insurgency capable—for now—only of engaging in small-scale guerrilla struggles. Communism was a universal creed: the appeal of both Communism and Fascism was much wider than al-Qaeda's, which can only hope to recruit the most alienated and temperamentally suited to its cause. Few who aren't already zealous Muslims will be converting to radical Islam.

Chapter 3

The Technique of a Coup-d'État

We discuss the information on coups to help us to understand what is going on today. From Ukraine to Lebanon via Kyrgyzstan, the iconography of revolution is always the same.

Indeed, many of the operatives of regime change under Ronald Reagan and George Bush Sr. have happily plied their trade in the former Soviet bloc under Bill Clinton and George Bush Jr. For instance, General Manuel Noriega reports in his memoirs that the two CIA-State Department operatives who were sent to negotiate and then engineer his downfall from power in Panama in 1989 were William Walker and Michael Kozak.

Walker resurfaced in Kosovo in January 1999 when, as head of the Kosovo Verification Mission, he oversaw the artificial creation of a bogus atrocity, which proved to be the *casus belli* for the Kosovo war while Michael Kozak became U.S. ambassador to Belarus, where in 2001 he mounted "Operation White Stork" designed to overthrow the incumbent President, Alexander Lukashenko. During an exchange of letters to *The Guardian* in 2001, Kozak brazenly admitted that he was doing in Belarus exactly what he had been doing in Nicaragua and Panama, namely "promoting democracy." There are essentially three branches to a modern technique of a coup—d'état. They are:

- ➤ non-governmental organizations
- ➤ control of the media
- ➤ covert operatives

Their activities are effectively interchangeable so I will not deal with them separately.

Serbia 2000—"People Power"

The overthrow of Slobodan Milosevic was obviously not the first time the West used covert influence to effect "regime change." The overthrow of Sali Berisha in Albania in 1997 and of Vladimir Meciar in Slovakia in 1998 were heavily influenced by the West and, in the case of Berisha, an extremely violent uprising was presented as a spontaneous and welcome example of people power. It was a classic example of how the international community, and especially the Organization for Security and Cooperation in Europe (OSCE), fiddled its election observation results in order to ensure political change. However, the overthrow of Slobodan Milosevic in Belgrade on the 5th of October 2000 is important because he is such a well-known figure, and because the "revolution," which unseated him involved a very ostentatious display of alleged "people power."

The background to the coup against Milosevic has been brilliantly described by British Sky TV. This account is valuable because it speaks approvingly of the events described; it is also interesting because it boasts of extensive contacts with the secret services, especially those of Britain and America. Here is part of the broadcast:

At every turn, the reporter seems to know who the main intelligence players are. His account is thick with references to "an MI6 officer in Pristina," "sources in Yugoslav military intelligence," "a CIA man who was helping to put together the coup," an "officer in U.S. naval intelligence" and so on. The reporter quotes secret surveillance reports from the Serbian secret police; the reporter knows who the Ministry of Defense desk officer is in London who draws up the strategy for getting rid of Milosevic; he knows that the British Foreign Secretary's telephone conversations are being listened to; he knows who are the Russian intelligence officers who accompany Yevgeni Primakov, the Russian prime minister to Belgrade during the NATO bombing; he knows which rooms are bugged in the British Embassy, and where the Yugoslav spies are who listen in to the diplomats' conversations; he knows that a staffer on the U.S. House of Representatives International Relations Committee is, in fact, an officer in U.S. Naval Intelligence; he seems to know that secret service decisions are often taken with the very minimal ministerial approval; he describes how the CIA physically escorted the Kosovo Liberation Army (KAL) delegation from Kosovo to Paris for the pre-war talks at Rambouillet, where NATO issued Yugoslavia with an ultimatum it knew it could only reject; and he refers to "a British journalist" acting as a go-between between London and Belgrade for hugely important high— level secret negotiations, as people sought to betray one another as Milosevic's power collapsed.

One of the themes which inadvertently run through the reporting is that there is a thin dividing line between journalists and spooks. Early on he refers casually to "the inevitable connections between officers, journalists and politicians," saying that people in all three categories "work in the same area."

The reporter then goes on jokingly to say that "a combination of "spooks," "journo's" and "politicos" added to "the people" 'were what had caused the overthrow of Slobodan Milosevic. He falls down by clinging to the myth that "the people" were involved, but the rest of his report shows that in fact the overthrow of the Yugoslav president occurred only because of political strategies deliberately conceived in London and Washington to get rid of him.' In short it had nothing to do with "people power."

Above all, the reporter makes it clear that, in 1998, the U.S. State Department and intelligence agencies decided to use the Kosovo Liberation Army to get rid of Slobodan Milosevic. He quotes one source saying, "The U.S. agenda was clear. When the time was right they were going to use the KLA to provide the solution to the political problem"—the "problem" being, Milosevic's continued political survival. This meant supporting the KLA terrorist secessionism, and later fighting a war against Yugoslavia on its side. The reporter quotes Mark Kirk, a U.S. naval intelligence officer saying: "Eventually we opened up a huge operation against Milosevic, both secret and open."

The secret part of the operation involved not only things like stuffing the various observer missions which were sent into Kosovo with officers from the British and American intelligence services, but also—crucially—giving military, technical, financial, logistical and political support to the KLA, which, as he himself admits, "smuggled drugs, ran prostitution rackets and murdered civilians." In short, the KLA was a group of thugs and killers.

The strategy began in late 1998 when 'a huge CIA mission (got) underway in Kosovo.' President Milosevic had allowed the Kosovo Diplomatic Observer Mission to enter Kosovo to monitor the situation in the province. It was a fatal mistake.

This ad hoc group was immediately stuffed with British and American intelligence agents and special forces—men from the CIA, U.S. Naval Intelligence, the British SAS and something called "14th intelligence," a body within the British army which operates side by side with the SAS to provide what is known as "deep surveillance."

The immediate purpose of this operation was "Intelligence Preparation of Battlefield"—a modern version of what the Duke of Wellington used to do, riding up and down the battlefield to get the lie of the land before engaging the enemy. Blucher thought it a waste of time but he was proved wrong. So as he puts it: 'Officially, the KDOM was run by the Organization for Security and Cooperation in Europe ... unofficially, the CIA ran (it)... The organization was just packed with them... It was a CIA front.'

Americans need to ask a lot of questions about this. Was the covert operation approved by the Congress and if so, on what grounds? If it was approved then it was in contravention to the U.S. Constitution and should never have been funded.

Many of the officers in fact worked for another CIA front, DynCorp, the Virginia-based company which employs mainly "members of U.S. military elite units, or the CIA." They used the KDOM, which later became the Kosovo Verification Mission for espionage. Instead of doing the monitoring tasks assigned to them, officers would go off and use their global positioning devices to locate and identify targets, which would be later bombed by NATO. Quite how the Yugoslavs could allow 2,000 highly trained secret service agents to roam around their territory is difficult to understand, especially since, Milosevic knew perfectly well what was going on. (End of quote)

The head of the Kosovo Verification Mission (KVM) was William Walker, the man sent to oust Manuel Noriega from power in Panama and a former ambassador to El Salvador whose U.S.-supported government ran death squads. Walker "discovered" the "massacre" at Racak in January 1999, the event which was used as a pretext for starting the process, which led to German Foreign Minister Joschka Fisher, called "Racak the turning point." Neither of these persons had much credibility at the time and even less today when their actions are weighed against what has since transpired.

As if to underscore the importance of Walker's account, the judges at The Hague tribunal allotted Walker nearly two days to testify. His "testimony" was *to* be the highlight of Milosevic's alleged role in the alleged Racak massacre, which opened the way to NATO's bombing of Yugoslavia. In contrast, when Milosevic asked how long he had to question the witness he was told by Judge May: *"Three hours, no more: if you refrain from arguing with the witness, if you refrain from repeating the question, if you ask short questions you will be able to get more done."* In spite this ghastly display of obvious bias on the part of

May, which in any other circumstances would have got him kicked off the bench, things did not turn out quite the way prosecutor Carla del Ponte expected.

William Walker was head of the Kosovo Verification Mission (KVM), which was set up under the control of the OSCE after an agreement between Milosevic and the U.S. envoy Richard Hollbrooke in October 13, 1998. Prior to his appearing at The Hague, two of Walker's weapons inspectors had given evidence about the events in Kosovo leading up to the NATO bombing— his deputy General Karol Drewienkiewicz and Colonel Richard Ciaglinski. They had also given evidence about the alleged massacre at Racak. What was the case against Milosevic?

On January 15, 1999, Serbian police and army personnel, accompanied by KVM inspectors and the media, mounted an operation against ethnic Albanian Kosovo Liberation Army (KLA) gunmen, whom they thought were hiding out in Racak following ambushing and killing three policemen. The army sent armored troop carriers and artillery into Racak, Petroovo, Malopoljce and Renaja. Two days later, after intense fighting between the Yugoslav forces and the KLA, Drewienkiewicz and Walker visited the area. Drewienkiewicz explained how on the way: *"Walker made it clear to me that I was to adopt an extremely uncompromising attitude in this matter."* When they arrived, the KLA took them to a gully that contained 45 dead bodies. No Serbians government officials were present during the "examination."

Once the bodies were uncovered, Drewienkiewicz told the court, *"Walker's assistant rushed to the top of a hill to phone through to NATO."* At a press conference that evening, Walker announced that there had been a massacre (without mentioning the deaths of the three policemen). Shortly before the announcement Drewienkiewicz said he heard Walker on the phone to Richard Hollbrooke saying: *"Dick, you can kiss your Nobel Peace Prize goodbye."* Drewienkiewicz added: *"I was surprised at the time that he was as specific as to refer to the event as a massacre. However, I do agree with what he said."*

Walker admitted that Drewienkiewicz had briefed him 14 hours before—the night of January 15 about fighting in the area between the KLA and the army and that three policemen had been killed in the vicinity three or four days before. He also knew on January 15 of police reports that 15 KLA militia had been killed at Racak, but at the press conference he said he disbelieved them. Film also shows him walking amongst KLA uniformed corpses.

Walker held his press conference on January 16 without mentioning the dead policeman or the KLA and saying that the bodies were all civilians. His press statement was, he said, "totally my creation." (Page 6805)

Walker admitted that he was "not a crime scene investigator" (page 6801) and when one arrived—Judge Danica Marinkovi - on January 17, he refused to meet her. During his testimony he said he had no recollection of Hollbrooke or NATO commander General Wesley Clark speaking to him—*"No recollection of myself talking to some of the people who have later said they talked to me."*

However, Wesley Clark does remember talking to Walker. In his book Clark describes a phone call from Walker on January 16: *"Wes, we've got trouble here,"* he began. *"I know a massacre when I see one. I've seen them before, when I was in Central America. And I am looking at a massacre now... There are forty of them in a ditch, maybe more. These aren't fighters, they're farmers, you can tell by looking at their hands and their clothes. And they have been shot at close range."*

Walker's account was disputed by the findings of a Finnish forensics team called in to investigate the incident. The team was firstly critical of the fact that, in the haste to describe the incident at Racak as a massacre, basic crime scene procedures had not been put into effect. Three days after the event, the Finnish forensic team reported that at no point was the scene of the incident isolated to stop unauthorized access. The report stated:

> Security and Cooperation Europe (OSCE) and European Union observers or the press.

Other findings show that only one dead victim was a woman. One victim was under 15 years of age. Six had suffered single gunshot wounds. Most of the 44 were covered by multiple wounds from different angles and elevations, characteristic of a firefight rather than a close range execution. Only one had been shot at close range and no signs of post-mortem mutilations were found. The team could not confirm that the victims were from Racak.

Compare Walker's attitude toward Racak with his attitude to the murder of six Jesuit priests in El Salvador or the killing of teenagers in Pec by the KLA. In El Salvador Walker tried to blame the killing of the Jesuits on guerrillas dressed as soldiers. He told the ICTY:

> "I made an inaccurate statement, in hindsight."

When the KLA was blamed for the killing of the Serb teenagers in Pec he said: "When you don't know what has happened, it's a lot more difficult to sort of pronounce yourself... To this day we do not know who committed that act." He did not exercise the same degree of caution regarding Racak.

When Milosevic tried to raise the events in El Salvador, Judge May intervened by saying: "Your attempt to discredit this witness with events so long ago the Trial Chamber has ruled as irrelevant." And later: "This is an absurd question, absolutely absurd. Now you're wasting everybody's time." Jurists may draw there own conclusions from the attitude of Mays whether or not he was fit to sit in judgment on the issues at hand.

Milosevic drew attention to the fact that Walker was at the same airport, Illopango, with Lt. Col. Oliver North who was gun running to the Contras, while Walker was supposedly providing them with humanitarian aid. Walker explained this by saying:

> Unbeknownst to me, unbeknownst to the State Department, unbeknownst essentially to the world, a Colonel Oliver North in the National Security Council was doing things that were eventually determined by Judge Walsh and his commission to be illegal.

Milosevic continued to try and discredit Walker's account and his interpretation of events in Racak.

He asked of Walker:

> Now that we are talking about Racak, in your statement you say the following: "As I was watching these bodies, I noticed a few things. First of all, judging by the wounds and the blood around them, and also the pools of dried blood on the land around the bodies; it was obvious that these were the clothes that the people wore when they were killed. There was no doubt in my mind that they died where they were lying. The quantity and the location of the blood on the soil in front of them, each and every one of them, was a clear indication of that".

Milosevic asked for a series of photos of the bodies to be shown in the correct order and asked:

> Where is this blood by the bodies or by individual bodies? Where did you see traces of blood there?

This began the following exchange:

Walker: *"On that picture?"*...

Milosevic: *"Are there any traces of blood here anywhere?"*

Walker: "*I assume that's blood.*"

Milosevic: "*You're talking about pools of blood on the soil, and on the soil there is no blood at all.*"

Walker: "*Not in this picture.*"

Milosevic: "*Not on the previous picture either. Is there any blood, any traces of blood, any pools of blood here on the soil either?*"

Walker: "*Not on that picture.*"

Milosevic: "*Not even here, there is no trace of blood anywhere on the ground, and we see that there are rocks all around.*"

Some of the photographs used in the trial came from one of Walker's observers in the KVM, a London Metropolitan police inspector, Ian Robert Hendrie, who had recently given evidence to the trial regarding his trip to the "massacre site."

When asked by Milosevic if he toured the site accompanied or alone, Hendrie said that someone had shown him around. He was asked whom and he replied: "*I don't know.*" Hendrie could not explain why his photographs showed only patches of blood and not pools. In his previous testimony, the chief forensic pathologist for the ICTY, Eric Baccard, admitted the stiffness and position of the dead bodies was unusual and it was possible they were moved. From the bullet wounds he said it was impossible to tell if they were due to "accident, homicide or an armed conflict."

In one incident, Milosevic asked Walker if he knew a Canadian Historian Roly Keith, who had been with NATO for 30 years and was head of the KVM in Kosovo Polje. Walker said he did not and so admitted that he could not remember his own head of KVM in Kosovo.

The reason for Walker's selective memory was apparent when Milosevic produced a quote from Keith which contradicted Walker's testimony as to the situation in Kosovo. Keith said:

> *I can testify to the fact that in February and March there was no genocide. When it comes to ethnic cleansing, I was not present nor did I see events which could be characterized as ethnic cleansing. In connection to my previous answer, I wish to state that I was witness to a series of incidents, and most of them were caused by the KLA, for which the security forces aided by the army reacted.*

Chapter 4

Prejudiced Court

Walker's silences and evasions over the activities of the KLA were again brought out when Milosevic asked if he had read the March 12, 2000 article in the *Sunday Times* entitled, "CIA aided Kosovo guerrilla army." Walker said he had not. The article explained how U.S. intelligence agents helped train the KLA before NATO's bombing of Yugoslavia. The CIA acted as ceasefire monitors in Kosovo in 1998 and 1999, while at the same time they were giving the KLA training manuals and field advice.

The article also questions Walker's role in preparing the way for NATO air strikes. "The American agenda consisted of their diplomatic observers, a.k.a. the CIA, operating on completely different terms to the rest of Europe and the OSCE, said a European envoy." While Walker dismissed claims that he wanted air strikes, he admitted that the CIA was involved in the countdown to them. Walker said:

> *Overnight we went from having a handful of people to 130 or more. Could the agency have put them in at that point? Sure they could. It's their job. But nobody told me.*

While no proof exists that Walker was a CIA agent, his role was in many respects no different from how the CIA operates. The article goes on to say that according to ex-CIA sources, diplomatic observers were "a CIA front, gathering intelligence on the KLA arms and leadership." One agent said: "I'd tell them which hill to avoid, which wood to go behind, that sort of thing." Klorin Krasniqi, a New York builder and one of the KLA's largest financiers said: *"It was purely the Albanian Diaspora helping their brothers."*

The article describes how the KLA got round a loophole that permitted sniper rifles to be exported to hunting clubs. Agim Ceku, a KLA commander, had established many contacts during the latter stages of the war through his work in the Croatian army. He said the Croatian army had been receiving help from an American company called Military Professional Resources Inc., whose personnel were in Kosovo at the time. Walker's testimony was another debacle for The Hague tribunal. Far too much information was released as to the real series of events that led up to the bombing of Serbia in 1999. Whether there was a massacre at Racak will need further study, although sufficient evidence has been shown for any objective observer to err on the side of caution. What is certain is that Walker played a pivotal role in providing NATO with justification for the bombing of Yugoslavia.

As Jacob de Haas, the biographer for Justice Brandeis, the U.S. Supreme Court Justice once wrote:

> *Government negotiations for deals of this nature, however, are always secret, and it is usually very difficult to obtain conclusive evidence at the time of the transaction. When the event is beyond repair and lost in the mists of the past, men are apt to write their memoirs and boast of secret exploits that once rocked the world.*

We do know that in spite of the dice being loaded against him by May and Carla del Ponte, Milosevic put up such a spirited defense that in the opinion of many observers, the court was made to look biased and prejudiced against him, giving little chance to disprove the allegations against him. Then, very mysteriously, under circumstances that appear to be highly suspicious, Milosevic was found dead in his cell, supposedly from natural causes.

But serious doubts about the cause of his death were raised by his doctor and his family. In spite of rigorous protests by his family, the verdict of death by natural causes remained in place.

Kozak and Walker Promote Revolutions

What emerges from the overthrow of the elected governments of Panama in 1989, Serbia 2000, Belarus 2001, Venezuela 2003, Georgia 2003, Ukraine 2004, Kyrgyzstan 2005 and Lebanon 2007 (ongoing) the connecting link is always the claim by the U.S. that the underlying principle is the "spread of democracy." I did a study of all of the abovementioned "revolutions" and the results were published in my monograph series, starting with the illegal give-away of the U.S. Canal at Panama and the overthrow of General Manuel Noriega.

The main tactics perfected in Panama were put into practice in Latin America during the 1970s and 1980s under the Reagan and George Herbert Walker Bush presidencies. It mattered not that these two U.S. presidents claimed to be "conservatives." Although not under the banner of "spreading democracy"— which was later changed to "regime change"—I make reference to it here to show that collusion between Britain and the United States is an integral part of the plans to advance the New World Order. The Thatcher-instigated and led British attack on the Falkland Islands was largely made possible by Reagan violating the Monroe Doctrine and materially assisting the British invasion force, again in violation of the U.S. Constitution.

In order for such strategic sabotage of civilian infrastructure in the political ream to succeed there has to be a cadre core of trained people on the ground to carry out the plan, and what emerged was that many of the operatives of regime change under Ronald Reagan and George Bush the elder, whether they were CIA, State Department operatives, or the vital media representatives, all had gained experience in the former Soviet bloc era under the presidencies of Clinton and George W. Bush.

General Manuel Noriega confirms this in his memoirs saying that the two CIA-State Department officers who were sent to Panama to bring about his downfall from power in 1989 were William Walker and Michael Kozak. Walker we have already met; in Honduras and El Salvador, and again, more recently in Kosovo in January 1999 when Clinton nominated him to run the so-called Kosovo Verification Mission.

Kozak was appointed America's ambassador to Belarus and using the embassy compound as his base against all diplomatic rules in 2001 fomented *"Operation White Stork"* to overthrow the incumbent President, Alexander Lukashenko. This was an echo of the operation mounted against Dr. Henrik Verwoerd of the Republic of South Africa, where the overthrow was managed by the U.S. embassy in Pretoria, from where all aid, comfort and huge financial largess was given to the Communist African National Congress (ANC) under the guise of bringing "democracy" to South Africa. The slogan "One Man One Vote" was probably the work of the Tavistock Institute. Kozak made it an open conspiracy when he wrote to *The Guardian* in 2001, admitting that what he was doing in Belarus was exactly what he had been doing in Nicaragua and Panama, namely "promoting democracy." The euphemism was used to cover a coup-d'état against countries not having the seal of approval of the New World Order.

Jeremy Bentham, one of the instigators and planners of the French Revolution (an early example of "bringing democracy" to France) was among the first practitioners of making the overthrow of the elected government of France a "people's movement."

Other essential elements needed for the success of a coup-d'état include deft sloganeering, ("Liberty Fraternity, Equality") ("One Man One Vote") non-governmental bodies, societies, and organizations, covert operatives on the ground and control of publicity through the media.

The Panama, Latin America and the former Soviet bloc country operations were beyond the conspiracy ventures of the New World Order. As we saw in Panama, Belarus and Serbia it was even advertised as such. In the case of Serbia it was broadcast far and wide by the media that the "revolution" was a "people power" demonstration. That was echoed again and again in the so-called "Orange Revolution " in the Ukraine. Serbia took a lot of managing and cooperation from supposedly "neutral" countries, particularly, Sweden.

It will be recalled, that Sweden had played a massive role in the return to Russia of Lenin and Trotsky and the financing of the Bolshevik Revolution, which was one of the firs supposed "People Power" revolutions. What this involved, as in the case of the ANC in South Africa, was giving very huge sums of money, as well as technical, logistical and strategic support, including arms, to various "democratic opposition" groups and "non- governmental organizations." In the Serbia operation, Walker and his associates worked principally through the International Republican Institute, supposedly a non-governmental private organization in Washington DC, which had opened offices in neighboring Hungary.

The money and all other necessities were brought into Serbia through diplomatic bags (a serious breach of diplomatic protocol). The pretense of neutrality as in the case of Sweden, being only one such example I cite, was maintained by not taking part NATO's illegal, criminal war against Serbia, thereby enabling it to maintain a full embassy in Belgrade on the spurious grounds that it was neutral.

I believe that NATO participation in the war against Serbia violated the following conventions and was thus, by any one or all of these conventions, is guilty of war crimes:

➢ The Nuremberg Protocols
➢ The four Geneva Conventions

> ➤ The United Nations Charter
> ➤ The European Union Convention
> ➤ The Hague Rules Governing Aerial Bombardment

Serbia is the only European country to be bombed since the end of WWII; hundreds of tons of bombs were dropped on mainly civilian infrastructure targets. As yet, the perpetrators of this war crime; President Clinton, General Wesley Clark, Madeline Albright, the NATO Generals, the President of the European Union and the UN Secretary-General have not yet been charged with war crimes. In the case of the Americans, additionally, they grossly violated the U.S. Constitution in five of its provisions (the highest law of the land) and under the provisions of the U.S. Constitution, should have been removed from office, impeached and tried for treason. Buying up media outlets is a principle ingredient needed for success in any coup-d'état. Allegedly "independent" media outlets such as Radio Station B92 were largely funded by U.S. organizations controlled and funded by George Soros who went on to play a crucial role in Ukraine and in Georgia. The so-called "democrats " constantly portrayed as such by the American and British jackals of the press, were foreign agents even as Milosevic had correctly stated. The political coup-d'état that defeated Milosevic began immediately after the first round of the presidential elections. What was presented on Western TV screens as "a spontaneous uprising of the people" consisted of a group of carefully selected extremely violent criminals and armed thugs under the command of Velimir Ilic, Mayor of the town of Cacak.

The 25-mile long convoy shown on its way to the federal parliament building in Belgrade, was not made up of citizens looking for democracy, but consisted of thugs, rowdies and paramilitary units of the "Black Pora" and a team of kick boxers. The fact of the matter is that on October 5th 2000 a virtual coup—d'état, was carefully hidden under the false facade of a people power revolution, and presented to the world as such by the running dogs of the media.

The next country to feel the dank breath of "people's democracy" was Georgia. The skills acquired and perfected in Panama, Honduras, Guatemala and Serbia, by now standard coup-d'état tactics, were put into action Georgia in November 2003 to overthrow President Edward Shevardnadze. The same false or distorted allegations were made and repeated over and over again following the "Big Lie" repetition perfected by Joseph Goebbels. The U.S. media, very much co-conspirators, while never bothering to check its facts, published allegations, that the voting was rigged although, astoundingly, the allegations were made long before the actual voting took place. A war of words was launched against Shevardnadze after a long period of having been idolized as a great reformer and democrat. As was the case with Belgrade, events were set in motion after a "storming of the parliament" took place and was dutifully broadcast live on TV.

Both transfers of power were brokered by the Russian minister, Igor Ivanov, who flew to Belgrade and Tbilisi to engineer the exit from power of the incumbent president. The role of Ivanov appears to have been Judas-like (especially since he was well known to both Shevardnadze and Milosevic of Serbia). Perhaps it was a case of an old score to settle with Shevardnadze? Another common denominator between Belgrade and Tiblisi was U.S. Ambassador Richard Miles.

Underhand civilian operations backed by huge sums of money in U.S. dollars played a key role in Georgia as it had done in Serbia. In both cases it was impossible to get details until long after the events had taken place before this vital information came out— thus of no use to undercut the massive anti-Shevardnadze propaganda about "people power" coming out in opposition to Shevardnadze. As is usual in such cases, the jackals of the media were careful to omit from printed media and television coverage, every incident, every scrap of information that supported Shevardnadze. In the case of Ukraine, we observe the same combination of work by Western-backed non-governmental organizations, the media and the secret services. The non-governmental organizations (NGO) played a huge role in delegitimizing the elections *before they even occurred.* Allegations of widespread fraud were constantly repeated. In other words, the street protests, which broke out after the second round, which Yanukovich won, were based on allegations, which had been doing the rounds *before the beginning of the first round.* The main NGO's behind these allegations, the Committee of Ukrainian Voters, received not one penny from Ukrainian voters, being instead fully funded by the United States. The National Democratic Institute was one of its main affiliates and it pumped out a steady stream of propaganda against Yanukovich.

During the events themselves, a neutral Spanish observer was able to document some of the propaganda abuses. They involved mainly the endless repetition of alleged electoral fraud practiced by the government; the constant cover-up of fraud practiced by the opposition; the frenetic selling of Viktor Yushchenko, one of the most boring men in the world, as charismatic as an Egyptian Mummy and the ridiculously unlikely story that he had been deliberately poisoned by his enemies. (No arrests and no charges were ever made in this fantasy case).

An interesting article by C. J. Chivers, published in *The New York Times* said that under the oversight of elements of American origin, the Ukrainian KGB had been working for Yushchenko for months before the so-called "people's uprising " took place. Details how military doctrine has been adapted to effect political change emerged (after the event) and that doctored "opinion polls" were used. The brainwashing methodology and the use of "inner directional condition" were according to the methodology of the Tavistock Institute of Human Relations.

In the foregoing accounts we have seen the New World Order's "diplomacy by deception"[1] in the conspiracy phase being

---

[1] Cf. *Diplomacy by Deception, An account of the treasonous conduct by the governments of Britain and the United States,* John Coleman,

enacted.

Much of what I have written was in many instances found right out in the open, showing that (at least in my opinion) the New World Order controllers no longer care whether the people discover their machinations or not—it is a conspiracy fact, an open conspiracy and it is as if the United States is proud of the leading role it is playing and cares not who knows it.

The Orange Revolution in Ukraine

Ukraine's Viktor Yanukovich, humiliated in the 2004 "Orange Revolution," was set to celebrate a political comeback as prime minister after his nemesis, President Viktor Yushchenko, supported him. The pro-Western Yushchenko, architect of the revolution that overturned the old order in Ukraine, reluctantly chose "co-habitation" with the Moscow-leaning Yanukovich in the early hours to end four months of political deadlock.

His only other real alternative had been to dissolve parliament, prolong the crisis and risk new elections that could have destroyed him politically. Yushchenko said he had decided to propose Yanukovich as prime minister of a coalition after extracting written guarantees that he would not try to overturn market reforms and pro-Western policies. There were no details on what concessions were made by Yanukovich, who favors closer ties with Russia, traditional ally of the ex-Soviet country. Parliament was expected to approve Yanukovich as prime minister later after his Regions party had signed a declaration of common principles with Yushchenko's "Our Ukraine" and other coalition parties. The deal ended four months of political deadlock in which Ukraine has had only a caretaker government. Apart from what concessions had been wrung from Yanukovich,

---

Omnia Veritas Ltd, www.omnia-veritas.com.

there were also questions over what grass-roots reaction there could be against Yushchenko from within his own "orange" ranks at doing a deal with Yanukovich. The charismatic and radical Yulia Tymoshenko, another big player in Ukraine who has been sidelined under the deal, had yet to show her hand.

Her political bloc finished second in a March parliamentary election, which Yanukovich's Regions party won easily. Though she could delay his appointment by a few hours, she did not have enough votes in parliament to block it. After hours of talks deep into the night trying to hammer out a coalition deal, Yushchenko said in a televised address: *"I have decided to put forward Viktor Yanukovich for the post of Ukraine's prime minister."* Yushchenko backed away from his other, high-risk option of dissolving parliament and calling new elections, choosing instead a potentially awkward "co-habitation" with Yanukovich. Pro- Russia candidate Viktor Yanukovych, the loser of the "orange revolution" presidential contest in 2004 is Ukraine's comeback kid. Written off by commentators after the revolution, he finally won the prime ministerial nomination after weeks of tortured negotiations. Yanukovych refused to slide into obscurity after he conceded defeat in a 2004 presidential election to his arch rival Viktor Yushchenko, who hundreds of thousands of demonstrators had come out to support when the result at first went Yanukovych's way.

Yanukovych won victory in that contest, but when massive "orange revolution" protests that seemed to erupt spontaneously in violent street demonstrations, the supreme court threw out the ballot because of allegations of wholesale fraud that had no basis in fact, and ordered a re-run of the election, which as expected Yushchenko won according to plan.

Abandoned by many of his allies, written off by the political elite, Yanukovych did something no one expected—he began playing by his orange foes' rules. With help from American consultants he adopted tactics used by his "orange" rivals in 2004. Deploying rock bands and plenty of blue-and-white paraphernalia for his campaign, he crossed the southeast shoring up grass-roots support. *"He was campaigning in 2004 as the crowned king,"* said a senior Western diplomat in Kiev during his campaign. *"He is campaigning now as a hungry politician.*

Chapter 5

Beyond the Conspiracy

D r. Howard Perlmutter, a professor of "Social Architecture" at the Wharton School and a follower of Dr. Emery (who) stressed that "rock video in Katmandu" was an appropriate image of how states with traditional cultures could be destabilized; thereby creating the possibility of a "global civilization."

There are two requirements for such a transformation, he added, "building internationally committed networks of international and locally committed organizations" and "creating global events" through "the transformation of a local event into one having virtually instantaneous international implications through mass-media." None of this is conspiracy theory—it is conspiracy fact.

The United States considers as a matter of official policy that the promotion of democracy is an important element of its overall national security strategy. Large sections of the State Department, the CIA, para-governmental agencies like the National Endowment for Democracy, and government-funded NGOs like the Carnegie Endowment for International Peace, which publishes several works on "democracy promotion."

All these operations have one thing in common: they involve the interference, sometimes violent of Western powers; especially the U.S. in the political processes of other states and that interference is very often used to promote the quintessential revolutionary goal and regime change. The current phase of the New World Order has been called "a period beyond the conspiracy" in that the managers of the New World Order, so emboldened by their latest successes that they do not care their plans have become quite transparent. One of the most notable ways a "beyond the conspiracy" phase can be determined is the new policy of creating revolutions (actually coup-d'état's) instead of mounting armed invasions of targeted countries. Apparently, the failure of the war in Vietnam, and the invasion of Iraq by the U.S. military in 1991 and again in 2002, has convinced the Committee of 300 that a coup-d'état is preferable to military conflict on the ground. This does not rule out air bombardments, but it has also been established that bombing alone, will not be enough to overcome the existing order of targeted countries, unless it can be in the magnitude of the mass bombing of Germany during 1944–1945. The successive "revolutions" breaking out all over the world, must be viewed in the foregoing context.

The new policy known as "beyond the conspiracy" was launched in real earnest in November 2003, the President of Georgia Edward Shevardnadze was overthrown following demonstrations, marches and allegations that the parliamentary elections had been rigged, which allegations were broadcast far and wide in the Western media even though no credible evidence was ever produced to substantiate voter fraud.

A year later, in November 2004, the so-called "Orange Revolution " was mounted in Ukraine with the same charges of widespread voter fraud charges that divided the country. There is a large pro-Russian population in the Ukraine and voter fraud would not have been necessary to maintain Ukraine's historical ties with Russia, but events of 2004—a virtual coup-d'état—put it on the path to becoming a permanent member of NATO and the EU.

The unofficial backers of the "Orange Revolution" and the jackals of the Western media, ensured that the so-called "people's revolution " would be a success. Allegations about voter fraud were actually mounted before any voting took place, the voter fraud allegations were repeated over and over again, the charge led by The Committee of Ukraine Voters, which was not funded by Ukrainians, but received every dollar of its funding from the United States. Did Soros play a role here?

It seems likely even if unproven. As if to advertise its origin, the walls of the offices of the committee were plastered with photographs of Madeleine Albright, the instigator and author of the revolution that overthrew the legitimate government of Serbia, while the National Democratic Institute fanned the flames with streams of volatile propaganda against the leading candidate, pro- Russia Vanukovi.

Chapter 6

Two Curious Men

The survival of the myth of spontaneous popular revolution is depressing because even a cursory examination of the facts found in written statements and various publications show this to be more than a myth, in fact, a blatant lie. Years ago, I received a copy of an account of the life of Curzio Malaparte, real name Kurt Sucker, the Italian writer, journalist and diplomat, who was born in Italy in 1898 and died in 1957. I studied the account as it seemed Mao Ts Tung had co-opted the idea of "people's revolution" from Malaparte.

Malaparte was a remarkable man with a remarkable knowledge of Europe and its politics, which came from first-hand experience as a diplomat and a correspondent for the prestigious Rome newspaper *Corriere della Serra*. He had covered the Eastern Front from Ukraine and his reports were later published under the name of *Volga Nasce in Europa* (The Volga Rises in Europe).

He was attached to U.S. General Mark Clark's invasion forces in Italy as a liaison officer and wrote a number of excellent articles about his experiences with the American Army. After the war, Malaparte joined the Italian Communist Party and later visited China after the "People's Republic of China" was established. After reading Malaparte's highly interesting life story, it seemed indeed that Mao could well have "borrowed" from Malaparte. Certainly, the U.S.-based organizations that were behind the so—called "Orange Revolution" had drawn on Malaparte's ideas, extensively, backed by unlimited money from Washington, (again, George Soros is suspected as the source, but not proven) and the more than willing cooperation of the Western media and the CIA. But it was probably Curzio Malaparte's *Technique of a coup-d'état,* which first gave very famous expression to these ideas. Published in 1931, this book presents regime change as just that—a technique.

Malaparte explicitly took issue with those who thought that regime change happened on its own. In fact, he starts the book by recounting a discussion between diplomats in Warsaw in the summer of 1920: Poland had been invaded by Trotsky's Red Army (Poland having itself invaded the Soviet Union, capturing Kiev in April 1920) and the Bolsheviks were at the gates of Warsaw.

The debate was between the British minister in Warsaw, Sir Horace Rumbold, and the Papal nuncio, Monsignor Ambrogio Damiano Achille Ratti—the man who was elected Pope as Pius XI two years later. The Englishman said that the internal political situation in Poland was so chaotic that a revolution was inevitable, and that the diplomatic corps therefore should flee the capital and go to Posen (Poznan).

Born in Prato, Tuscany, to a Lombard mother and a German father, he was educated at Collegio Cicognini and at the La Sapienza University of Rome. In 1918 he started his career as a journalist.

Malaparte fought in World War I, earning a captaincy in the Fifth Alpine Regiment and several decorations for valor, and in 1922 took part in Benito Mussolini's March on Rome. In 1924, he founded the Roman periodical La Conquista dello stato ("The Conquest of the State," a title which would inspire Ramiro Ledesma Ramos' La Conquista del Estado). As a member of the Partito Nazionale Fascista, he founded several periodicals and contributed essays and articles to others, as well as writing numerous books, starting from the early 1920s and directing two metropolitan newspapers.

In 1926 he founded with Massimo Bontempelli (1878–1960) the literary quarterly 900. Later he became a co-editor of Fiera Letteraria (1928-31) and an editor of La Stampa in Turin. His confessional war novel, *La rivolta dei santi* (1921), criticized corrupt Rome as the real enemy. In *Tecnica del colpo di Stato* (1931) Malaparte attacked both Adolf Hitler and Mussolini. This led to Malaparte being stripped of his National Fascist Party membership and sent to internal exile from 1933 to 1938 on the island of Lipari.

He was freed on the personal intervention of Mussolini's son— in— law and heir apparent Galeazzo Ciano. Mussolini's regime arrested Malaparte again in 1938, 1939, 1941 and 1943 and imprisoned him in Rome's infamous jail—Regina Coeli. Shortly after his time in jail he published books of magical realist autobiographical short stories, which culminated in the stylistic prose *of Donna Come Me* (Woman Like Me) (1940).

His remarkable knowledge of Europe and its leaders is based upon his experience as a correspondent and in the Italian diplomatic service. In 1941 he was sent to cover the Eastern Front as a correspondent for *Corriere della Sera*. The articles he sent back from the Ukrainian Fronts, many of which were suppressed, were collected in 1943 and brought out under the title Il *Volga nasce in Europa* ("The Volga Rises in Europe"). Also, this experience provided the basis for his two most famous books, *Kaputt* (1944) and *The Skin* (1949).

Kaputt, his novelistic account of the war, surreptitiously written, presents the conflict from the point of view of those doomed to lose it. Malaparte's account is marked by lyrical observations, as when he encounters a detachment of Wehrmacht soldiers fleeing a Ukrainian battlefield:

> *When Germans become afraid; when that mysterious German fear begins to creep into their bones, they always arouse a special horror and pity. Their appearance is*

*miserable, their cruelty sad, and their courage silent and
hopeless.*

Malaparte extends the great fresco of European society he began
in *Kaputt*. There the scene was Eastern Europe, here it is Italy
during the years from 1943 to 1945; instead of Germans; the
invaders are the American armed forces.

In all the literature that derives from the Second World War there
is no other book that so brilliantly or so woundingly presents
triumphant American innocence against the background of the
European experience of destruction and moral collapse. The
book was condemned by the Roman Catholic Church and placed
on the Index Librorum Prohibitorum.

From November 1943 to March 1946, he was attached to the
American High Command in Italy as an Italian Liaison Officer.
Articles by Curzio Malaparte have appeared in many literary
periodicals of note in France, the United Kingdom, Italy and the
United States.

After the war, Malaparte's political sympathies veered to the left
and he became member of the Italian Communist Party. In 1947
Malaparte settled in Paris and wrote dramas without much
success. His play *Du Cote de chez Proust* was based on the life
of Marcel Proust, and Das Kapital was a portrait of Karl Marx.
Cristo Proibito ("Forbidden Christ") was Malaparte's
moderately successful film—which he wrote, directed and
scored in 1950.

It won the "City of Berlin" special prize at the Berlin Film
Festival in 1951. In the story, a war veteran returns to his village
to avenge the death of his brother, shot by the Germans. It was
released in the United States in 1953 as *Strange Deception* and
voted among the five best foreign films by National Board of
Review. He also produced the variety show *Sexophone* and
planned to cross the United States on bicycle.

Just before his death, Malaparte completed the treatment of another film, Il *Compagno P.* After the establishment of the People's Republic of China in 1949, Malaparte became interested in the Maoist version of Communism, but his journey to China was cut short by illness, and he was flown back to Rome.

Io in Russia e in Cina, his journal of the events was published posthumously in 1958. Malaparte's final book, *Maledetti toscani,* his attack on bourgeois culture, appeared in 1956. He died of cancer.

This anecdote allows Malaparte to discuss the differences between Lenin and Trotsky, two practitioners of the coup-d'état/revolution. Malaparte shows that the future Pope was right and that it was wrong to say that pre-conditions were necessary for a revolution to occur. For Malaparte, as for Trotsky, regime change could be promoted in any country, including the stable democracies of Western Europe, providing that there was a sufficiently resolute body of men determined to achieve it. There is no doubt that the techniques of Malaparte were followed to the letter in Yugoslavia, Ukraine and Georgia.

This description of Malaparte and his ideas is relevant to what the United States did in Panama, Honduras, Nicaragua, Yugoslavia; U.S. relations with Mao Tse Tung, the invasion of Iraq and the ongoing war of words with Iran. His thoughts and ideas are being used by the new Left (Neo-Conservatives) to bring about revolution in the U.S., which is a lot closer than most think.

This brings us onto a second body of literature, concerning the manipulation of the media. Malaparte himself does not discuss this aspect, but it is (a) of huge importance and (b) clearly a subset of the technique of a coup-d'état in the way regime change is practiced today. So important, indeed, is the control of the media during regime change that one of the main characteristics of these revolutions is the creation of a virtual reality. Control of this reality is itself an instrument of power, which is why in classic coups in a banana republic the first thing that the revolutionaries seize is the radio station.

People experience a strong psychological reluctance to accept that political events today are deliberately manipulated. This reluctance is itself a product of the ideology of the information age, which flatters people's vanity and encourages them to believe that they have access to huge amounts of information. In fact, the apparent multifarious nature of modern media information hides an extreme shortage of original sources, rather as a street of restaurants on an Italian waterfront can hide the reality of a single kitchen at the back.

News reports of major events very often come from a single source, usually a wire agency, and even authoritative news outlets like the BBC simply recycle information, which they have received from these agencies, presenting it as their own. BBC correspondents are often sitting in their hotel rooms when they send dispatches, very often simply reading back to the studio in London information they have been given by their colleagues back home off the wire.

A second factor which explains the reluctance to believe in media manipulation is connected with the feeling of omniscience which the mass media age likes to flatter: to garbage news reports as manipulated is to tell people that they are gullible, and this is not a pleasant message to receive.

There are many elements to media manipulation. One of the most important is political iconography. This is a very important instrument for promoting the legitimacy of regimes, which have seized power through revolution. One only need think of such iconic events as the storming of the Bastille on 14th July 1789, the storming of the Winter Palace during the October revolution in 1917, or Mussolini's March on Rome in 1922, to see that events can be elevated into almost eternal sources of legitimacy.

However, the importance of political imagery goes far beyond the invention of a simple emblem for each revolution. It involves a far deeper control of the media, and generally this control needs to be exercised over a long period of time, not just at the moment of regime change itself. It is essential indeed, for the official party line to be repeated *ad nauseam*. A feature of today's mass media culture which many dissidents lazily and wrongly denounce as "totalitarian" is precisely that dissenting views may be expressed and published, but this is precisely because, being mere drops in the ocean, they are never a threat to the tide of propaganda.

One of the modern masters of such media control was the German Communist from whom Joseph Goebbels learned his trade; Willi Munzenberg. Munzenberg was not only the inventor of spin, he was also the first person who perfected the art of creating a network of opinion-forming journalists who propagated views, which were germane to the needs of the Communist Party in Germany and to the Soviet Union. He also made a huge fortune in the process, since he amassed a considerable media empire from, which he creamed off the profits. Munzenberg was intimately involved with the Communist project from the very beginning. He belonged to Lenin's circle in Zurich and in 1917 accompanied the future leader of the Bolshevik revolution to the Zurich Hauptbahnhof, from whence Lenin was transported in a sealed train and with the help of the German imperial authorities, to the Finland Station in St. Petersburg. Lenin then called on Munzenberg to combat the appalling publicity generated in 1921 when 25 million peasants in the Volga region started to suffer from the famine, which swept across the newly created Soviet state.

Munzenberg, who had by then returned to Berlin, where he was later elected to the Reichstag as a Communist deputy was charged with setting up a bogus workers' charity, the Foreign Committee for the Organization of Worker Relief for the Hungry in Soviet Russia, whose purpose was to pretend to the world that humanitarian relief was coming from sources other than Herbert

Hoover's American Relief Administration. Lenin feared not only that Hoover would use his humanitarian aid project to send spies into the USSR (which he did), but also, perhaps even more importantly, that the world's first Communist state would be fatally damaged by the negative publicity of seeing capitalist America come to its aid within a few years of the revolution.

After having cut his teeth on "selling" the death of millions of people at the hands of the Bolsheviks, Munzenberg turned his attention to more general propaganda activities. He amassed a large media empire, known as "the Munzenberg trust," which owned two mass circulation dailies in Germany, a mass circulation weekly and which had interests in scores of other publications around the world. His greatest coups were to mobilize world opinion against America over the Sacco-Vanzetti trial (two anarchist Italian immigrants who were sentenced to death for murder in Massachusetts in 1921) and to counteract the Nazis' claim in 1933 that the Reichstag fire was the result of a Communist conspiracy.

The Nazis, it will be remembered, used the fire to justify mass arrests and executions against Communists, even though it now appears that the fire genuinely was started on his own by the man arrested in the building at the time, the lone arsonist Martinus van der Lubbe. Munzenberg actually managed to convince large sections of public opinion of the equal but opposite untruth to that peddled by the Nazis, namely that the Nazis had started the fire themselves in order to have a pretext for removing their main enemies.

The key relevance of Munzenberg for our own day is this: he understood the key importance of influencing opinion-formers. He targeted especially intellectuals, taking the view that intellectuals were especially easy to influence because they were so vain. His contacts included many of the great literary figures of the 1930s, a large number of whom were encouraged by him to support the Republicans in the Spanish Civil War and to make that into a *cause-celebre* of Communist Anti-Fascism.

Munzenberg's tactics are of primary importance to the manipulation of opinion in today's New World Order. More then ever before, so-called "experts " constantly pop up on our TV screens to explain what is happening, and they are always vehicles for the official party line. They are controlled in various ways, usually by money, flattery or academic recognition.

There is a second body of literature, which makes a slightly different point from the specific technique which Munzenberg perfected. This is about the way in which people can be made to react in certain collective ways by psychological stimuli.

This is the basis upon which the Tavistock Institute of Human Relations operates. Perhaps the first major theoretician of this was Sigmund Freud's nephew, Edward Bernays, who worked at Tavistock and whose book *Propaganda* in 1928 said that it was entirely natural and right for governments to organize public opinion for political purposes. The opening chapter of his book has the revealing title, *"Organizing chaos."*

Bernays writes:

> *The conscious and intelligent manipulation of the organized opinions and habits of the masses is an important element in democratic society. Those who manipulate this unseen mechanism of society constitute an invisible government, which is the true ruling power of our country.*

Bernays says that, very often, the members of this invisible government do not even know who the other members are. Propaganda, he says, is the only way to prevent public opinion descending into dissonant chaos. This is also what Malaparte believed. Bernays continued to work on this theme after the war, editing *Engineering Consent* in 1955, a title to which Edward Herman and Noam Chomsky alluded when they published their seminal *Manufacturing Consent* in 1988.

The connection with Freud is important because, as we shall see later, psychology is an extremely important tool in influencing public opinion. Two of the contributors to *Engineering Consent* make the point that every leader must play on basic human emotions in order to manipulate public opinion.

For instance, Doris E. Fleischmann and Howard Walden Cutler write:

> *Self-preservation, ambition, pride, hunger, love of family and children, patriotism, imitativeness, the desire to be a leader, love of play—these and other drives are the psychological raw materials which every leader must take into account in his endeavor to win the public to his point of view... To maintain their self-assurance, most people need to feel certain that whatever they believe about anything is true.*

This was what Willi Munzenberg understood—the basic human urge for people to believe what they want to believe. Thomas Mann alluded to it when he attributed the rise of Hitler to the collective desire of the German people for "a fairy tale" over the ugly truths of reality of defeat in the First World War although not defeated in the field. Other books worth mentioning in this regard concern not so much modern electronic propaganda but the more general psychology of crowds. The classics in this regard are Gustave Le Bon's work, *The Psychology of Crowds* (1895), Elias Canetti's, *Crowds and Power (Masse und Macht)* (1980); and Serge Tchakhotine's, *Le Viol des Foules par la Propagande Politique* (1939).

All these books draw heavily on psychology and anthropology. There is also the magnificent oeuvre of one of my favorite writers, the anthropologist Rene Girard, writing on the logic of imitation (mimesis), and on collective acts of violence, are excellent tools for understanding why it is that public opinion is so easily motivated to support war and other forms of political violence. After the war, many of the techniques perfected by the Communist Munzenberg were adopted by the Americans, as has been magnificently documented by Frances Stonor Saunders' excellent work, *Who Paid the Piper?*, published in America under the title, *The Cultural Cold War.*

In minute detail, Stonor Saunders explains how, as the Cold War started, the Americans and the British started up a massive covert operation to fund anti-Communist intellectuals. The key point is that much of their attention and activity was directed at left— wingers, in many cases Trotskyites who had abandoned their support for the Soviet Union only in 1939, when Stalin signed his non-aggression pact with Hitler, and in many cases people who had previously worked for Munzenberg. Many of the figures who were at this juncture between Communism and the CIA at the beginning of the cold war were future neo-conservative (Bolshevik) lights, especially Irving Kristol, James Burnham, Sidney Hook and Lionel Trilling.

The left-wing and even Trotskyite origins of neo-conservatism are well-known—even if I still continue to be astonished by new details I discover, such as that Lionel and Diana Trilling were married by a rabbi for whom Felix Dzerzhinsky (the founder of the Bolshevik secret police, the Cheka (forerunner of the KGB), and the Communist equivalent of Heinrich Himmler) represented a heroic paragon.

These left-wing origins are particularly relevant to the covert operations discussed by Stonor Saunders, because the CIA's goal was precisely to influence left-wing opponents of Communist, i.e. Trotskyites. The CIA's view was simply that right-wing anti-Communists did not need to be influenced, much less paid. Stonor Saunders quotes Michael Warner when she writes:

> For the CIA, the strategy of promoting the Non-Communist Left was to become "the theoretical foundation of the Agency's political operations against Communism over the next two decades."

This strategy was outlined in Arthur Schlesinger's *The Vital Center* (1949), a book which represents one of the cornerstones of what was later to become the Neo-Bolshevik movement:

> *The purpose of supporting leftist groups was not to destroy or even dominate, but rather to maintain a discreet proximity to and monitor the thinking of such groups; to provide them with a mouthpiece so that they could blow off steam; and, in extremis, to exercise a final veto over their actions, if they ever got too "radical."*

Many and varied were the ways in which this left-wing influence was felt. The U.S. was determined to fashion for itself a progressive image, in contrast to the "reactionary" Soviet Union. In other words, it wanted to do precisely what the Soviets were doing. In music, for instance, Nicholas Nabokov (the cousin of the author of "Lolita") was one of the Congress' main agents. In 1954, the CIA funded a music festival in Rome in which Stalin's "authoritarian" love of composers like Rimsky-Korsakov and Tchaikovsky was "countered" by unorthodox modern music inspired by Schoenberg's twelve-tone system later used to promote the Beatles. *"For Nabokov, there was a clear political message to be imparted by promoting music which announced itself as doing away with natural hierarchies...*

Support for other progressives came when Jackson Pollock, himself a former Communist, was also promoted by the CIA. His daubs were supposed to represent the American ideology of "freedom" over the authoritarianism of socialist realist painting.

(This alliance with Communists pre-dates the Cold War. The Mexican Communist muralist, Diego Rivera, was supported by Abby Aldrich Rockefeller, but their collaboration ended abruptly when Rivera refused to remove a portrait of Lenin from a crowd scene painted on the walls of the Rockefeller Center in 1933).

This cross-over between culture and politics was explicitly promoted by a CIA body, which went under an Orwellian name, the Psychological Strategy Board. In 1956, it covertly promoted a European tour by the Metropolitan Opera, the political purpose of which was to encourage multiculturalism. Junkie Fleischmann, the organizer, said:

> We, in the United States, are a melting-pot and, by being so, we have demonstrated that peoples can get along together irrespective of race, color or creed. Using the "melting-pot" or some such catch phrase for a theme we might be able to use the Met as an example of how Europeans can get along together in the United States and that, therefore, some sort of European Federation is entirely practicable.

This, by the way, is exactly the same argument employed by, among other people, Ben Wattenberg, whose book *The First Universal Nation* argues that America has a special right to world hegemony because she embodies all the nations and races of the planet. The same view has also been expressed by Newt Gingrich and other Neo-Conservatives. Other themes promoted include some which are at the forefront of Neo-Bolshevik thinking today. First among these is the eminently liberal belief in moral and political universalism. Today, this is at the very heart of George W. Bush's own foreign policy philosophy; he has stated on numerous occasions that political values are the same all over the world and he has used this assumption to justify U.S. military intervention in favor of "democracy."

Back in the early 1950s, the director of the PSB (the Psychological Strategy Board was quickly referred to only by its initials, no doubt in order to hide its real name), Raymond Allen, had already arrived at this conclusion:

> The principles and ideals embodied in the Declaration of Independence and the Constitution are for export and ... are the heritage of men everywhere. We should appeal to the fundamental urges of all men which I believe are the same for the farmer in Kansas as for the farmer in Punjab.

To be sure, it would be wrong to attribute the spread of ideas only to covert manipulation. They have their force in large-scale cultural currents, whose causes are multiple. But there is no doubt that the dominance of such ideas can be substantially facilitated by covert operations, especially since people in mass-information societies are curiously suggestible.

Not only do they believe what they have read in the papers, they also think they have arrived at these conclusions themselves. The trick of manipulating public opinion, therefore, lies precisely in that which Bernays theorized, Munzenberg initiated, and which the CIA raised to a high art. According to CIA agent Donald Jameson:

> *As far as the attitudes that the Agency wanted to inspire through these activities are concerned, clearly what they would like to have been able to produce were people who, of their own reasoning and conviction, were persuaded that everything the United States government did was right.*

To put it another way, what the CIA and other U.S. agencies were doing during this period was to adopt the strategy, which we associate with the Italian Marxist, Antonio Gramsci, who argued that "cultural hegemony" was essential for socialist revolution.

Finally, there is a huge body of literature on the technique of disinformation. I have already referred to the important fact, originally formulated by Tchakotine (Chakotin), that the role of journalists and the media is key in ensuring that propaganda is constant: *"Propaganda cannot take time off,"* he writes, *"thereby formulating one of the key rules of modern disinformation, which is that the required message must be repeated very frequently indeed if it is to pass."* Above all, Tchakotine (Chakotin) says that propaganda campaigns must be centrally directed and highly organized, something which has become the norm in the age of modern political "spin;" British Labor Members of Parliament, for instance, are not allowed to speak to the media without first asking permission from the

Director of Communications in 10 Downing Street.

Sefton Delmer was both a practitioner and theoretician of such "black propaganda." Delmer created a bogus radio station, which broadcasted from Britain to Germany during the Second World War and which created the myth that there were "good" patriotic Germans who opposed Hitler. The fiction was sustained that the station was actually an underground German one, and was put on frequencies close to those of official stations. Such black propaganda has now become part of the U.S. government's armory of "spin;" the *New York Times* revealed that the U.S. government makes news reports favorable to its policies, which are then carried on normal channels and presented as if they were the broadcast company's own reports.

There are many other such authors, some of whom I have discussed. Curzio Malaparte is the one most overlooked in the West largely because so few know about him. But perhaps the most relevant to today's discussion is Roger Mucchielli's book, *Subversion*, published in French in 1971, which shows how disinformation had moved from being an auxiliary tactic in war to a principal one. The strategy had developed so far, he said, that the goal was now to conquer a state without even attacking physically, especially through the use of agents of influence inside it.

This is essentially what Robert Kaplan proposed and discussed in his essay for *The Atlantic Monthly* in July/August 2003:

> *"Supremacy by Stealth." One of the most sinister theoreticians of the New World Order and the American empire, Robert Kaplan, explicitly advocates the use of immoral and illegal power to promote U.S. control of the whole world. His essay deals with the use of covert operations, military power, dirty tricks, black propaganda, hidden influence and control, opinion-forming and other things like political assassination, all subject to his overall call for "a pagan ethic," as the means to ensuring American*

domination.

The other key point about Mucchielli is that he was one of the first theoreticians of the use of bogus non-governmental organizations—or "front organizations" as they used to be known—for effecting internal political change in another state. Like Malaparte and Trotsky, Mucchielli also understood that it was not "objective" circumstances which determined the success or failure of a revolution, but instead the perception created of those circumstances by disinformation. He also understood that historical revolutions, which invariably presented themselves as the product of mass movements, were in fact the work of a tiny number of highly organized conspirators.

In fact, again like Trotsky, Mucchielli emphasized that the silent majority must be rigorously excluded from the mechanics of political change, precisely because coups d'état are the work of the few and not the many.

Public opinion was the "forum" in which subversion was practiced, and Mucchielli showed the different ways in which the mass media could be used to create a collective psychosis. Psychological factors were extremely important in this regard, he said, especially in the pursuit of important strategies such as the demoralization of a society. The enemy must be made to lose confidence in the Tightness of his own cause, while all effort must be made to convince him that his adversary is invincible.

Chapter 7

The Role of the Military

O ne final historical point before we move on to part II, a discussion of the present, and that is the role of the military in conducting covert operations and influencing political change. This is something which some contemporary analysts are happy to admit is deployed today: Robert Kaplan writes approvingly of how the American military is, and should be, used to "promote democracy." Kaplan says that a phone call from a U.S. general is often a better way of promoting political change in a third country than a phone call from the local U.S. ambassador. And he approvingly quotes an Army Special Operations officer saying:

> *Whoever the President of Kenya is the same group of guys run their special forces and the President's bodyguards. We've trained them. That translates into diplomatic leverage.*

The historical background to this has recently been discussed by a Swiss academic, Daniele Glaser, in his book, *Nato's Secret Armies.*

His account begins with the admission made on 3rd August 1990 by Giulio Andreotti, the then Italian Prime Minister, that a secret army had existed in his country since the end of the Second World War, known as "Gladio;" that it had been created by the CIA and MI6 and that it was coordinated by the unorthodox warfare section of NATO.

Here again; the writings of Curzio Malaparte are overlooked in the West.

Glaser thereby confirmed one of the most long-running rumors in post-war Italy. Many people, including investigating magistrates, had long suspected that Gladio was not only party of a network of secret armies created by the Americans across Western Europe to fight in the resistance to a putative Soviet occupation, but also that these networks had become involved in influencing the outcome of elections, even to the extent of forming sinister alliances with terrorist organizations. Italy was a particular target because the Communist Party was so strong there.

Originally, this secret army was constructed with the aim of providing for the eventuality of an invasion. But it seems that they soon moved to covert operations aimed at influencing the political process itself, in the absence of an invasion. There is ample evidence that the Americans did indeed interfere massively, especially in Italian elections, in order to prevent the PCI from ever winning power. Tens of billions of dollars were funded to the Italian Christian Democrats by the U.S. for this very reason.

Glaser even argues that there is evidence that Gladio cells carried out terrorist attacks in order to blame Communists and to frighten the population into demanding extra state powers to "protect" them from terrorism. Glaser quotes the man convicted of planting one of these bombs, Vincenzo Vinciguerra, who duly explained the nature of the network of which he was a foot soldier.

He said that it was part of a strategy *"to destabilize in order to stabilize:"*

> *You had to attack civilians, the people, women, children, innocent people, unknown people far removed from any political game. The reason was quite simple. They were supposed to force these people, the Italian public, to turn to the state to ask for greater security. This is the political logic*

*which remains behind all the massacres and the bombings
which remain unpunished, because the state cannot convict
itself or declare itself responsible for what happened.*

There is an obvious relevance to the conspiracy theories swirling
around 9/11. Glaser presents a host of good evidence that this is
indeed what Gladio did, and his arguments shed light on the
intriguing possibility that there might also have been an alliance
with extreme left wing groups like the Red Brigades. After all,
when Aldo Moro was kidnapped, shortly after which he was
assassinated, he was physically on the way to the Italian
parliament to present a program for a coalition government
between the Socialists and the Communists—precisely the thing
the Americans were determined to prevent.

The new phase of the New World Order has been called "a period
beyond the conspiracy" in that the managers of the New World
Order are so emboldened by their latest successes, that they do
not care that their plans have become quite transparent. One of
the most notable ways the "beyond the conspiracy" phase can be
determined is by searching what documents there are covering a
new policy for the managers of the New World Order; the
creating of revolutions (actually coup-d'état) instead of mounting
armed invasions of targeted countries. Here again Curzio
Malaparte's writings seem to underpin everything.

Apparently, the failure of the war in Vietnam, and the invasion
of Iraq by the U.S. military in 1991 and again in 2002, has
convinced the Committee of 300 that a coup-d'état is preferable
to military conflict on the ground. This does not rule out air
bombardments, but it has also been established that bombing
alone, will not be enough to overcome the existing order of
targeted countries, unless it can be in the magnitude of the mass
bombing of Germany during 1944–1945.

The successive "revolutions" breaking out all over the world,
must be viewed in this light. The new policy known as "beyond

the conspiracy" was launched in real earnest in November 2003, the President of Georgia Edward Shevardnadze was overthrown following demonstrations, marches and allegations that the parliamentary elections had been rigged, which allegations were broadcast far and wide in the Western media even though no credible evidence was ever produced to substantiate voter fraud.

A year later, in November 2004, the so-called "Orange Revolution " was mounted in Ukraine with the same charges of widespread voter fraud charges that divided the country. There is a large pro-Russian population in the Ukraine and voter fraud would not have been necessary to maintain Ukraine's historical ties with Russia, but events of 2004—a virtual coup-d'état put it on the path to becoming a permanent member of NATO and the EU.

The survival of the myth of spontaneous popular revolution is depressing, because even a cursory examination of the facts found in written statements and various publications show this to be more than a myth, I would venture to say, a blatant lie. Certainly, the U.S.-based organizations that were behind the so-called "Orange Revolution " had drawn on Malaparte's ideas, extensively, backed by unlimited money from Washington, and the more than willing cooperation of the Western media and the CIA was wrong to say that pre-conditions were necessary for a revolution to occur. For Malaparte, as for Trotsky, regime change could be promoted in any country, including the stable democracies of Western Europe, providing that there was a sufficiently resolute body of men determined to achieve it.

> *"For the CIA, the strategy of promoting the Non-Communist Left was to become 'the theoretical foundation of the Agency's political operations against Communism over the next two decades.'*

This strategy was outlined in Arthur Schlesinger's *The Vital Center* (1949), a book which represents one of the cornerstones of what was later to become the neo-conservative movement.

Stonor Saunders writes:

> *The purpose of supporting leftist groups was not to destroy or even dominate, but rather to maintain a discreet proximity to and monitor the thinking of such groups; to provide them with a mouthpiece so that they could blow off steam; and, in extremis, to exercise a final veto over their actions, if they ever got too 'radical.'*

Many and varied were the ways in which this left-wing influence was felt. The USA was determined to fashion for itself a progressive image, in contrast to the 'reactionary' Soviet Union. But perhaps the most relevant to today's discussion is Roger Mucchielli's book, *Subversion*, published in French in 1971, which shows how disinformation had moved from being an auxiliary tactic in war to a principal one.

The strategy had developed so far, he said, that the goal was now to conquer a state without even attacking physically, especially through the use of agents of influence inside it. This is essentially what Robert Kaplan proposed and discussed in his essay for *The Atlantic Monthly* in July/August 2003, 'Supremacy by Stealth.'

One of the most sinister theoreticians of the New World Order and the American empire, Robert Kaplan, explicitly advocates the use of immoral and illegal power to promote U.S. control of the whole world. His essay deals with the use of covert operations, military power, dirty tricks, black propaganda, hidden influence and control, opinion-forming and other things like political assassination, all subject to his overall call for 'a pagan ethic,' as the means to ensuring American domination.

Chapter 8

The Shame of Iraq

The erosion of a target country's integrity and viability has always been a conscious goal of the Western colonial project. Creating instability and dissatisfaction with existing reality was a necessary prerequisite to 'tame' and then integrate native peoples into the dominant hierarchical model. Today, of course, we are told that colonialism is a thing of the past. The leading nations of the international community no longer seek to enslave their less fortunate neighbors, but rather pursue policies of world benefaction—within the limits imposed by healthy competition, of course. When this miraculous conversion took place we are not told, but perhaps it occurred incrementally, parallel to the increasing divide between the world rich and poor. In any case, a casual glance at the state of the Muslim world is enough to shatter this foolish delusion.

As Iraqi society descends further and further into mayhem, comedians and commentators of all kinds have made great hay from the supposed incompetence and stupidity of our leaders. But as the *Canadian Spectator* suggested recently, if it should happen that the United States is not run by buffoons, *'one must conclude that chaos, impoverishment and civil war in the Muslim world ... far from being the unintended consequences, are precisely the objectives of U.S. policy.'*

The reason for the current state of affairs is that as I have just stated, the Committee of 300 has moved out of the shadow of the world-wide conspiracy, out into the open, beyond the conspiracy. There is no longer any pretense; a New World Order inside a One World Government is the openly declared goal. As with 9/11, the trigger event for the War on Terror, incompetence is the preferred explanation for the nightmare scenario in Iraq today. Though counterintuitive to the domesticated populations of the West, a plan to deliberately fragment Iraq along ethnic lines is amply confirmed by the published record. Resuscitating earlier Zionist schemes, the U.S. Council on Foreign Relations recently called for the dissolution of the 'unnatural Iraqi state.' On the grounds of its ethnic diversity, Iraq is said to be a false, artificial construct, a product of arbitrary colonial decisions in the early 20th century. It is a judgment that could apply to many of the world's countries and yet the theme is being enthusiastically adopted by reams of 'experts' who would never dream of questioning state sovereignty in Quebec, the Basque Country or Northern Ireland. In typical fashion, Neo-Bolshevik policy— analyst Michael Klare recently dismissed Iraq as an 'invented' country:

> ... to facilitate their exploitation of oil in the region the British created the fictitious 'Kingdom of Iraq' by patching together three provinces of the former Ottoman Empire ... and by parachuting in a fake king from what later became Saudi Arabia.

Accepting the Bush Administration's bogus rationale for the invasion, Klare ascribed Sunni resistance to the desire for a bigger share of oil revenues in the future partition of the country. Missing is any idea that resistance extends beyond 'Sunnis' or could be motivated by Iraqi nationalism or the need for self-determination. Ultimately, the ease with which Western academics casually decide to reshape the countries of their choice owes itself to the continuing legacy of the Committee of 300.

In classic nineteenth century style, the chattering heads suggest that Iraq, despite its five thousand-year history, is now incapable of managing itself and so its fate must be decided by outside powers. A country that held together in 1991 through six weeks of the most intensive bombing campaign in history, (which according to the UN left Iraq in a 'pre-industrial age') and continued to survive through 12 years of the most completely brutal and devastating sanctions ever imposed on any nation, is now blithely consigned to history by so-called Western experts. To bolster their case, the myth of ancient sectarian hatreds, a staple of the 'humanitarian intervention' gangsters is rehashed and fed on a daily basis by journalists who neither question the authorship of 'sectarian' attacks nor report the view of ordinary Iraqis, (who blame the occupation army and its puppet government for the orchestrated chaos).

The preparations for the occupation of Iraq began almost immediately after the first assault in 1991. We should add that with this illicit attack called 'Desert Storm' not sanctioned by the U.S. Constitution and which found no authority in Emmerich Vattel's *Law of Nations,* the 'Bible' on which the U.S. Constitution draws heavily, the United States fell off the precipice into a canyon of barbarism rivaling anything seen in the Middle Ages, or even later in the Mongol invasion of Europe.

'Desert Storm' was lawless banditry at its worst, for which the United States is destined to pay a high price. With the arbitrary imposition of no-fly-zones in the north and south of the country on the sole say-so of George Bush the elder, in flagrant violation of international law and the U.S. Constitution, and with the profane concurrence of the western media already dividing the country into three mutually antagonistic regions, the stage was set for one of the worst atrocities to befall any country in ancient and modern history.

The first indication of what was to come was the organized sacking of museums (170,000 pieces lost) and burning of libraries following the fall of the Government of Saddam Hussein in 2003. Later, when the Occupation forces" first chief, General Jay Garner, recommended maintaining the Iraqi military and creating a coalition government, defense secretary Rumsfeld removed him. His successor, Paul Bremer, went on to dismantle the army and other key national institutions, as well as "losing" some $9 billion of Iraq's oil revenues along the way.

The reconstituted puppet army was formed almost exclusively from the Kurdish and Shi'ite communities. Meanwhile, anonymous assassins began targeting Iraq's academic community, eventually provoking a huge "brain drain" from the country and further debilitating the country's capacity to recover. When the armed opposition groups became active in the country, there followed a string of events bearing the hallmarks of undercover operations designed to stoke up sectarian conflict and taint the Iraqi Resistance. What follows is a brief summary of the most suspicious incidents.

A truck bomb tore through UN headquarters four months into the occupation, killing special envoy Sergio Vieira de Mello and 19 others, pro-consul Bremer suggested two possible culprits: "Saddam loyalists or foreign insurgents." The interim government's Ahmed Chalabi, however, had received prior notice of the attack the week before. Chalabi had been warned that a "soft target" was to be attacked, although it would be "neither the Coalition Authority nor coalition troops." But the UN, whose security had been withdrawn that day, was never warned.

By November 2003, with the guerilla campaign inflicting heavy losses on U.S. forces, the media and interim governing authority began a steady drumbeat of sectarian brainwashing. After weeks of scare mongering about a civil war, coordinated explosions left 143 Shi'ite civilians dead in Kerbala and Baghdad. The blame fell on "al Qaeda," but journalist Robert Fisk asked the obvious question:

> "If a violent Sunni group wished to evict the Americans from Iraq ... why would it want to turn the Shi'ite population ... 60 per cent of Iraqis, against them?"

No answer was provided, and the senseless attacks increased.

In early February 2004 American authorities claimed to have

intercepted a message from Iraq asking "al Qaeda" for help in fomenting a civil war. Almost immediately, as if to underline the message, an explosion killed 50 Shias in the small town of Iskandariya. "Terrorists spark fear of civil war," announced *The Independent*, contradicting the town's residents who, without exception, attributed the blast to an American air strike. "They heard a helicopter overhead and the whoosh of a missile just before the blast."

The blast itself left a crater five-feet deep, more consistent with a missile than a car bomb.

As with the parent organization, nothing about this group rings true. Until 2004 "al Qaeda," a Sunni-only set up, had never uttered a word against Shi'ites. But as the Iraqi Resistance campaign gained unstoppable momentum, the reportedly deceased Jordanian militant Abu Musab Zarqawi suddenly resurfaced. Calling for war against the "infidel" Shi'ite community, he went on to wage a parallel campaign characterized more by gratuitous attacks on civilians than by ejecting the U.S. from Iraq.

In the following years, wherever the U.S. unleashed massive assaults in Iraq, Zarqawi was conveniently "discovered" to be hiding. The November 2004 assault on Fallujah was waged with white phosphorous and left at least 6,000 dead beneath the ruins, and yet US surveillance was so sharp that Zarqawi, with his one wooden leg, was apparently observed fleeing on the first day! Amongst Iraqis, the all-purpose Zarqawi was referred to as a kind of mobile WMD able to appear wherever required. His story remained incredible right up to the end, the released photo evidence showing the lightly bruised body of a man killed with a 500lb bomb. Truth is certainly stranger than fiction when it comes to the multiplicity of contrived situations that occur in Iraq on an almost daily basis.

By April of 2004 the game was well and truly up. Fallujah

became the first major town to come under the open control of the Resistance. Simultaneously, U.S. repression provoked an uprising by the Shi'ite Mehdi Army and the U.S. found itself waging a war on two fronts. Massive shows of inter-faith solidarity ensued with 200,000 Sunnis and Shi'ites on April 9th gathering for collective prayers in Baghdad's largest Sunni mosque, where the lead preacher derided the possibility of civil war as an American pretext for extending the occupation.

The U.S. faced a chorus of protest around the world as it bludgeoned Fallujah from the air in a desperate attempt to retake the city. Then, photographs of systematic torture in the Abu Ghraib detention center were released to the press, finishing off what little credibility the U.S. retained in world opinion. Detracting from the negative publicity, however, previously unknown militant groups began kidnapping foreign nationals and releasing gruesome videos in which the kidnap victims were frequently beheaded on camera when the kidnappers' demands were not met.

The first victim was businessman Nick Berg, in an alleged "retaliation" for Abu Ghraib. The killing, said to be the work of al Zarqawi, came under scrutiny when independent media questioned the execution tape's veracity. It was determined that the video had first been uploaded to the Internet from London, and after examination of the images by a Mexican forensic surgeon, many observers agreed that the man shown in the film was already a corpse when beheaded.

Anglo-Irish aid worker Margaret Hassan had lived in Iraq for 30 years and dedicated her life to the welfare of Iraqis in need, fighting tirelessly against UN sanctions and opposing the Anglo-American invasion. So when she was kidnapped on her way to work in the autumn of 2004, Iraqis were incredulous. Spontaneous public information campaigns were started and a poster showing Hassan holding a sick Iraqi child appeared on billboards across the capital. "Margaret Hassan is truly a daughter of Iraq," it read. Patients of Iraqi hospitals took to the streets in protest against the hostage takers, and prominent Resistance groups, even including the phantom Zarqawi, called for her release.

Her kidnappers did not issue any specific demands, but in the captivity video Hassan pleaded for the withdrawal of British troops. In previous cases, the groups had identified themselves and used the videos to make their demands. But Margaret Hassan's kidnapping was different from the start. This group used no specific name and no banners or flags to identify itself. In their videos appeared none of the usual armed and hooded men or Koran recitations. Other abducted women, were released "when their captors recognized their innocence." But not in the case of Hassan, even though she spoke fluent Arabic and could explain her work to her captors in their own language. A video soon surfaced purporting to show her execution and an Iraqi man, Mustafa Salman al-Jubouri, was later sentenced to life imprisonment by a Baghdad court for aiding and abetting the kidnappers. To this date, no group has ever claimed responsibility.

Long after piles of corpses began appearing by the roadsides, victims of anonymous assassins, *Newsweek* magazine reported on a Pentagon plan to use counterinsurgency death squads to eliminate Iraqi Resistance fighters and their supporters. The so— called 'Salvador Option' named after a similar campaign in Central America in the 1980s, was confirmed by later reports of Interior ministry involvement in the burgeoning death squads. As the victims mounted, the corporate media filtered the story through its angle of Sunni fanatics targeting innocent Shi'ite civilians. But the facts showed a different story. According to a report by the Center for Strategic and International Studies, the bulk of resistance attacks (75%) were on Coalition Forces, far exceeding that of any other category in their survey (with attacks organized by quantity, type of target, and numbers killed and wounded).

In sharp contrast to the corporate media's picture, civilian targets comprised a mere 4.1% of attacks. After 300,000 Baghdad Shias staged the largest popular demonstrations since 1958, M. Junaid Alam asked:

> *"Would such a massive number of Shiites have shown up to protest the occupation if they thought that most of the Sunni-based armed resistance, also opposed to the occupation, was trying to kill them?"*

2005 saw a spectacular rise in the use of car bombs, many directed against innocent civilian targets. Though the Zarqawi network was said to have no more than about a thousand men in Iraq, it apparently had an endless supply of personnel ready to sacrifice their lives for the holy war. Other accounts, however, suggest a different explanation.

In May 2005, former Iraqi exile Imad Khadduri, reported how a driver whose license had been confiscated in Baghdad was questioned for half an hour at an American military camp, informed that there were no charges against him, and then directed to the al-Khadimiya police station to retrieve his license.

> *The driver did leave in a hurry, but was soon alarmed with a feeling that his car was carrying a heavy load, and he also became suspicious of a low flying helicopter that kept hovering overhead, as if trailing him. He stopped the car and found nearly 100 kilograms of explosives hidden in the back seat, the only feasible explanation for this incident is that the car was indeed booby trapped by the Americans and intended for the al-Khadimiya Shiite district of Baghdad. The helicopter was monitoring his movement and witnessing the anticipated "hideous attack by foreign elements."*

(According to Khadurri, the scenario was repeated again in Mosul, when a driver's car broke down on the way to the police station where he was sent to reclaim his license. He then turned to discover the spare tire to be laden with explosives).

In the same month, 64-year-old farmer Haj Haidar, who was taking his tomato load from Hilla to Baghdad, was stopped at an American checkpoint and had his pick-up thoroughly searched. Allowed to go on his way, his 11 year-old grandson then told him he saw one of the American soldiers placing a grey melon-sized object amidst the tomato containers.

Realizing the vehicle was his only means of work; Haidar fought his initial impulse to run and removed the object from his truck, placing it in a nearby ditch. He later learnt that it had in fact exploded, killing part of a passing shepherd's flock of sheep.

At this point, legendary Iraqi reporter "Riverbend" wrote that many of the supposed suicide bombings were in fact remotely detonated car bombs or time bombs. She related how a man was arrested for allegedly having shot at a National Guardsman after huge blasts struck in west Baghdad. But according to the man's neighbors, far from having shot anyone, he had seen:

> ... an American patrol passing through the area and pausing at the bomb site minutes before the explosion. Soon after they drove away, the bomb went off and chaos ensued. He ran out of his house screaming to the neighbors and bystanders that the Americans had either planted the bomb or seen the bomb and done nothing about it. He was promptly taken away.

In Basra on September 19th, 2005, suspicious Iraqi police stopped undercover British soldiers in a Toyota Cressida. The two men then opened fire, killing one policeman and wounding another. Eventually captured, they were identified by the BBC as members of the SAS elite Special Forces. The soldiers were in wigs and dressed as Arabs and their car was packed with explosives and towing equipment. Fattah al-Shaykh, a member of the Iraqi National Assembly, told Al-Jazeera TV that the car was meant to explode in the centre of Basra's popular market. Before his thesis could be confirmed, however, the British army's tanks flattened the local prison cell and freed their sinister operatives. Plans to orchestrate sectarian chaos became more obvious in the Occupation's third year. In one incident, the Baghdad police told commanders of the Shi'ite Mehdi Army that gunmen near the village of Madain were holding 150 Shi'ite civilians hostage.

When the militia sent fighters to the area to negotiate their release, they were fired upon, losing at least 25 men. "I think it was a set-up; the fire was too heavy," said an aide to the Mehdi militia, adding the attackers used snipers and heavy machine guns. Local townspeople were unaware of the supposed hostage crisis and no hostages were ever discovered there. Although the incessant sectarian brainwashing was clearly having an effect, Iraqis continued to dismiss the idea of a civil war.

In the wake of the destruction of Samarra's Golden Mosque, however, the scale of the killing in Iraq rose sharply. Those responsible for this critical attack wore Iraqi National Guard uniforms according to the mosque guards. Joint forces of Iraqi ING and Americans, patrolling the surrounding area the whole while, went on to assist a militia attack on a Sunni mosque in a pre-programmed "response."

The response of most ordinary Iraqis however was quite different, According to Sami Ramadani:

> None of the mostly spontaneous protest marches were directed at Sunni mosques. Near the bombed shrine itself, local Sunnis joined the city's minority Shias to denounce the occupation and accuse it of sharing responsibility for the outrage. In Kut, a march led by Sadr's Mahdi army burned U.S. and Israeli flags. In Baghdad's Sadr City, the anti-occupation march was massive.

The Western media, however, could now seize upon each and every incident as evidence of an irreparable social disintegration. Columnist Daniel Pipes approvingly observed that sectarian conflict would reduce attacks on U.S. forces as Iraqis fought each other. His comments were then reflected on Fox News with onscreen captions that read: "Upside To Civil War?" and "All—Out Civil War in Iraq: Could It Be a Good Thing?"

The key to justifying the horrendous colonial assault on Iraq was the non-stop manufacture of propaganda. Although not provable, there must have been someone in the Bush administration that had studied Curzio Malaparte.

Cheerleader Thomas Freidman had likened Saddam's Iraq to an ethnically segregated Alabama in the era of lynching. Shia and Kurds were held as subhuman.

Although the Minister of Health was Kurdish and the government had two Shia Prime ministers (Sadoun Humadi and Mohammed Al-Zubaidi), that the Vice President was a Christian, never intruded on Freidman's "analysis." In fact, Iraqis rarely asked about the religion or ethnicity of the leaders and functionaries they reported to. It was simply not a matter of concern for them.

Meanwhile, for the "human rights" brigade, propagandists such as *The Independent's* Johann Hari would hash out a two-dimensional caricature of a country in which a hellish regime murdered, each year, 70,000 of its own citizens (without anyone really noticing). In spite of the Ba'ath government's admitted crimes, however, a visitor could pass through Baghdad in the 1990s without coming across tanks, car bombs, kidnappings, air strikes, fuel shortages power, cuts and vast detention gulags. And whatever the scale of Saddam's crimes, they are pale next to those of the American Occupation Forces.

Saddam had no intention of dismantling the government, the army, civic institutions; of looting the museums and killing the teachers and intellectuals, of ethnic cleansing the Christians and the Sunnis and inciting violence between the sects. Saddam had no plan to increase malnutrition, to reduce the flow of clean water, to cut off the electricity, to remove the social-safety net, to increase the poverty and unemployment, or to set Iraqi against Iraqi in a vicious struggle for survival.

Saddam did not abide by the neoconservative theory of "creative destruction," which deliberately plunged an entire nation into chaos destroying the fabric of Iraqi society and leaving the people to flock to militias for safety. The truth is that the approaching peak of global oil production threatens to fatally weaken the U.S. power bloc.

Hence, Saddam's Iraq, an independent, oil-rich state in the most strategically important region on Earth could not be allowed to survive. But the intractable resistance to the Occupation has obligated the U.S. to turn to its contingency plan (officially, of course, it didn't have one). In this plan, something similar to Oded Yinon's tripartite balkanization of the country is being thrashed out. Existing independent states are to be broken up and replaced by a cluster of weak and pliant protectorates.

The particulars may be very different, but the engineered breakup of Yugoslavia undoubtedly serves as the model for this dismemberment. "In *the 1990s,*" wrote Diana Johnston,

> "*the U.S.-led International Community was no longer interested in state-building. Nation-state deconstruction was more compatible with economic globalization measures.*"

To this end, in Iraq as in Yugoslavia, the U.S. has allied itself with "state-splitters" and sectarian bigots, all the while publicly claiming to uphold national sovereignty. In case of any misunderstanding, Neo-Bolshevik ideologues have clarified matters: "natural" sectarian tensions, they say, will inevitably arise in the absence of a repressive state to subdue them. Therefore, under their benevolent guidance, Iraq must be allowed to devolve into its ethnic components.

After the 1991 bombing of Iraq and George Bush Sr.'s announcement of a "New World Order" of American hegemony, foreign policy forums effectively proclaimed the nation-state obsolete. In fact, the global imposition of the Western model of development after WWII had already ended the traditional independence of the State. The "new" ideology was simply recognition of facts on the ground. After the Soviet collapse, celebrated advocates of the anti-nation-state ideology predicted an approaching "End of History," which would see all the world's peoples integrate into a global, urban, capitalist and consumer lifestyle.

Thus, the "chaotic diversity of cultures, values and beliefs that lay behind the conflicts of the past" would be removed in a general process of political and cultural homogenization. It is still too early to predict the end of this delirious vision, but across the world, people are opting to forge their own future, increasingly deaf to the advice of the super elites. In Iraq, consciousness of the big picture is greater than anywhere else.

Thus, the planned breakdown into generalized sectarian conflict has not materialized. As the armed resistance intensifies its struggle against the U.S. and openly confronts the Salafi Jihadist terrorists, a pendant has become extremely popular amongst Iraqis. Seen on the streets and on television, anchorwomen wear it while reading the news. The pendant has the form of Iraq.

When TV stations showed Kalashnikov-wielding teenagers going toe-to-toe with the world's most powerful army in Fallujah, the images evoked a struggle of epochal significance. But alongside the armed resistance, journalists, intellectuals, trade unionists and Iraqis of all walks of life are, each on their own terrain, facing off against military-corporate rule.

Chapter 9

Blueprint for Wars Beyond the Conspiracy

As in all so-called "crisis situations, " the "crisis" came about as a result of a contrived situation. The sinking of the Lusitania, the Japanese attack on Pearl Harbor and the alleged torpedo boat attacks on the U.S. fleet in the Gulf of Tonkin that opened the way for President Johnson to send U.S. forces to Vietnam are prime examples. I hope I demonstrated that the unprovoked attack on Yugoslavia was another in a line of such contrived situations as was the 2001 attack on Iraq on the pretext of Iraq's imaginary possessions of "Weapons of Mass Destruction." I can think of no better way for the truth to be told about what happened in the run- up to the Clinton-ordered war on Yugoslavia, than from the late President Milosevic.

First regarding the late President Milosevic; the descriptions in the Western press were off the mark; intelligent, calm and dignified, a man who knew who he was and didn't have to advertise himself.

Unlike Albright, whose father was held responsible for stealing a valuable art collection belonging to the owner of the apartment he was renting, Milosevic's honesty was commented on by several neutral representatives of foreign governments who said he always conducted himself with confidence, and dignity.

In explaining what happened, the late Slobodan Milosevic made it abundantly clear who were the instigators of the war on Serbia:

Yugoslavia was a modern federation with different cultures, heritages, living with little discord and the question of who is Macedonian, who is Croatian, etc., was imposed from the outside especially by the American Holbrook. It was only at that point did problems arise. No people having an interest in their welfare would start agitating for the dissolution of Yugoslavia, when a part of the Croatian people was living in Bosnia and so on? Or Muslims? And what would become of us, divided into little states?

In Europe there is no recognition of cultural and ethnic differences. Every country needs new formulas adapted to deal with cultural and ethnic differences in a respectful fashion. Yugoslavia had such a code. NATO is supposedly an alliance. An alliance means equal states. But in fact, NATO was a war machine imposed by the U.S. Big Master. It's understandable for the USA, as the most powerful nation, to aspire to a leading role. Americans could have been benevolent. But instead you chose the path of Caesar, spreading blood and killing nations. So you missed the millennium, not just the century. It would be comic if it wasn't tragic.

Everything has become transparent. Consider this very brief history. In October 1997, leaders of the Southeast European countries met, all of us. We established a very good understanding. I suggested, "Let's do something for ourselves. Let's abolish customs fees among ourselves." The meeting was very good. I had excellent person to person discussions with Fatos Nano, the Albanian Prime Minister. We discussed opening our borders and he said Kosovo is an internal problem of our country. The message of that meeting was that in Southeast Europe things are going to be solved by mutual consultation. A month later I received a letter from German Foreign Minister Klaus Kinkle and French Foreign Minister Hubert Vedrine, stating that they were very concerned about Albanians. And then of course the BND [German intelligence] organized the so-called UCK [KLA] in 1998. They started to shoot, to kill postmen, foresters; they threw bombs in cafes, near green markets. We reacted as any state would react. By summer of 1998 they were gone, destroyed. At that point Balkans Envoy] Richard Hollbrooke came here to insist that his armed personal be allowed into Kosovo—as observers, he said: We talked. Our discussions were frustrating. We would solve a problem one day and Hollbrooke would re-open it the next. I would say, "But we solved that problem yesterday!" And he would say, "Instructions." He wanted to send in 20,000 armed so-called observers. This was accompanied by the threat that NATO would bomb us.

We tried to minimize the harm of this blackmail, to rouse world public opinion. At the same time we whittled down Holbrooke's demands from 20,000 to 2000, and from armed to unarmed so— called observers. So, it was something less than outright armed invasion. Though still an assault on our sovereignty. They put a criminal, William Walker, in charge of their observers. This is a man who worked with death squads in El Salvador. Supposedly a diplomat, his observers were mostly intelligence operatives, behind the veneer of a private American company DynCorp. Like Lockheed, DynCorp gets all of its money from government and military contracts. It is a private spy agency that supplies information to the Pentagon and a variety of other U.S. Government agencies

Walker created Racak, the phony massacre, based on his El Salvador expertise. Racak was then used by Madeleine Albright to justify their ultimatum to negotiate at Rambouillet. We were told: negotiate or be bombed. Of course, under international law, no treaty that results from threats is legally binding. But that wasn't their concern. We decided to use these supposed negotiations to illustrate our stand. Our delegation was a composite of our national groups. It included ethnic Serbs, Albanians, Gorani [Slavic Muslims], Roma ["Gypsies"], Turks. The composition of Kosovo before the UCK [Kosovo Liberation Army] drove most of them out. Meanwhile, the complete text of the Rambouillet "agreement" appeared in an Albanian publication three days before our delegation even arrived in France. Do you see? It was drawn up in advance. So our delegates read the thing. One showed it to the Americans, saying, "Look, this is badly done. It's garbage." And one of the Americans said, "What are you talking about? It was prepared by James O 'Brien! One of our best men! He drew up the complete documents for the autonomy of Tibet!' That's what we had to deal with. And what of Clinton? He actually said Serbs were responsible for W.W.I and W.W.II. An Israeli newspaper asked me if the anti-Serb media demonizing was a form of genocide. After all, the demonizing was used to justify the air war, which involved almost exclusively bombing of civilians, destroying normal life, the life of a people.

The Serbs are the only Europeans who have been bombed since World War II. 22,000 tons of bombs were dropped. Without the avalanche of media lies, ordinary Western citizens would never have allowed it. So the demonizing was a crucial part of the war machine, limiting international protest. It was part of the genocide. People in the NATO countries are not yet aware they were lied to. And they aren't aware how much harm this has done to their societies. Clinton's administration put lies into an ostensibly democratic institutional apparatus thus preventing any possibility of democracy. How can people make choices when they're basing their thinking on lies?

The destruction of Yugoslavia is material proof that the U.S. and other forces are engaged in a new colonialism. If their big words about world integration were true, they would have preserved Yugoslavia. It embodied precisely such integration. Nobody can be against integration if it is just, if people are treated equally. The new colonialism consists in making the small part richer, the big part poorer; and killing nations. If you lose your country, your independence and freedom, all other battles are lost. How can you organize a country for prosperity when you don't have a country? If we understand that we're facing a new type of colonialism, one that attacks national sovereignty, we can pull all our forces together. The Left once grasped this idea, which is why Imperial forces penetrated the Left.

Now the Left is often worse than the Right. In Germany they removed Kohl and put in Schroeder, who will do anything for the Americans. Gorbachev was an American guy as well. He destroyed the Soviet Union for them. For years the Russians have functioned as if under hypnosis.

The Americans succeeded in hypnotizing them into believing their economy depends on the IMF and the World Bank. Hundreds of billions have been taken out of Russia; the lives of ordinary people are destroyed; and they waste time negotiating IMF loans.

Consider the possibilities. The whole of Western Europe is relying on natural gas production. Why wasn't Russia the big supplier? It could if the Russians had that in mind instead of playing this fool's game of relying on the IMF. Look at the economic models the IMF enforces! Kenneth Galbraith, the American economist, said: 'If the Americans deployed these economic models in America they 'd be destroyed.' The question for Russians is: When will you realize the need and possibility to be your own masters? There is no way to play the Americans" game and win. The USA controls the entire international banking system.

I have been attacked for everything. The U.S. envoy, Richard Hollbrooke, once told me, the Swiss government is going to freeze your accounts. I said: "Why stop there? Here, wait a moment." I wrote a few words and gave him the paper. "Here. I've signed all my foreign bank account assets over to you. You may keep every penny."

He was taken aback. "I may?" I said, "Yes! Unfortunately, there are no accounts." Generally in banking you cannot have presidents of countries hiding vast amounts of money. It's simply nonsense. The goal of all the news reports about how they haven't yet found my money is to give people the false impression that there's something to look for.

A private citizen on a Serbian TV station was criticizing the media, and right in the middle, the station cut the power. Just like that. The screen went black. It shows how worried this DOS regime [installed in a coup-d'état in October 2000] is when faced with the least critical thought. They accuse me of having been a dictator. That's ridiculous. Before the DOS coup-d'état we had democracy. 95% of the media was privately owned and the opposition controlled most of it. In Kosovo the Albanians had more than 20 different media. In any neighborhood you could buy a newspaper attacking the government. We didn't have one political prisoner. But this new regime has issued so-called "amnesty" laws, freeing members of the KLA convicted for murdering children and the like. They call this "the new political freedom." I call it legalizing terror. How did my supposed dictatorship manifest itself? Ibrahim Rugova, the Albanian secessionist leader, could have a press conference in Belgrade. He could walk around freely, have lunch, and criticize everything. And he did. Nobody bothered him.

They've accused me of being behind a rash of killings that occurred before the coup-d'état. The Defense Minister was killed. The Prime Minister of the province of Vojvodina was killed. The Secretary General of the Yugoslav Left, the Deputy Interior Minister of Serbia, the Managing Director of Yugoslav Airlines, a friend of mine since Gymnasium, he was killed. These were people I worked with, friends. No opposition leader was killed. So, I was killing my friends and sparing my enemies. A unique strategy.

When a crime occurs, shouldn't one ask: Qui bono? [Who gains?] Isn't it obvious that these killings were carried out to benefit our foreign opponents? That they were an attempt to intimidate men and women in our government? But the Western—controlled media says I was responsible.

The opposition media demonized our government and me and my family in every possible way. They accused my son of being a criminal. The TV mixed these slanders with programs imported from America; flashy images, seductive especially to young people. They are doing this all over the world. It is a cultural attack.

Of course it had some effect. People in our country aren't used to advertising techniques based on the repetition of false images. The opposition learned these techniques from their U.S. and other NATO handlers. I've been using the term "opposition," but in fact we had no opposition. We had a

Fifth Column. It was paid huge sums by the people who bombed us.

This was openly admitted. And this Fifth Column, who now occupies government positions, has gone so far as to agree to cooperate with The Hague Tribunal, a false Tribunal created as another part of the genocide against the Serbs. Once in awhile they arrest an Islamic Fundamentalist or a Croatian fascist, to imply balance. But the goal is to destroy those who uphold Yugoslavia, who defend Serbia, to leave ordinary people vulnerable to attack and to make the world think resistance is impossible.

This past week the current authorities in Belgrade shipped their first victim to The Hague. He is a Serb from Bosnia, active in refugee work. And we are seeing Hague-type justice in Belgrade as well. The present authorities have arrested Dragoljub Milanovic, the director of RTS [the State TV station].

This is how it went. In January, Hague Prosecutor, Carla del Ponte, came to Belgrade. She accused me and Dragoljub Milanovic of murder. Why? Because on April 23, 1999, NATO bombed RTS, killing 16 people in one of their cruelest bombing raids. And, she said, NATO had made it clear they would bomb; so by her mad logic, we were responsible. On April 8th French officials did threaten to bomb RTS. On the 9th, we surrounded the TV station with a human shield, journalists, managers, officials, all together, arms linked. Serbian citizens were doing the same on bridges and in factories, everywhere.

Then Wesley Clark seemed to withdraw the threat, but in any case what were we to do? Not go to work? Employees occupied our biggest auto plant and wrote a letter appealing to NATO not to bomb. NATO bombed anyway, killing and wounding scores of people. Were the victims guilty? Mr. Milanovic was working at RTS all month and could have been killed as well. Would that have made him responsible for 17 deaths, instead of 16? Of course, Carla del Ponte works for NATO, for the bombers. And the new Belgrade authorities who actually arrested Dragoljub Milanovic on this crazy charge, these people work for NATO too. War crimes—who is guilty?

There were war crimes in Kosovo. But by who? By the terrorists, who committed atrocities as a matter of course; by NATO, which never hurt our military? They bombed our homes. They dropped cluster bombs on our green markets. Bombs encased in uranium. These are war crimes. And they are guilty of the greatest crime of all: they launched an illegal, aggressive war. Their actions now, everything they do, is intended to hide the criminal responsibility of Clinton, Albright, Blair, Schroeder, Solana, all the others.

They are the worst war criminals. But they accuse me. They say I ordered the slaughter of Albanians in Kosovo. And to prove it they sent forensic experts all over Kosovo, looking for atrocities. This was a propaganda effort, not a scientific investigation. It was theater—for the media. Every step these experts took was reported: they are looking for the bodies; they will soon unearth the bodies; they have found a shoe; and so on.

With all that, people had to assume: there must be some serious crimes here. The news that they were looking was big news but the news that they had found nothing—that was very small news. It is my opinion that many people in your countries still believe we committed genocide against Albanians in Kosovo.

At the end of May 1999 the Russians proposed to us the so-called Yeltsin peace plan. It was good. Then it appears the Russians met with the Americans in Finland, and when the Russian envoy, Victor Chernomyrdin arrived in Belgrade the plan was entirely different. Kosovo was said to remain a part of Yugoslavia, but the plan also called for full withdrawal of Yugoslav forces and for UN occupation. We said how do we know this will not turn into NATO occupation and [KLA] terror? Chernomyrdin swore to us that our Russian brothers would not permit this.

What were we to do? On the one hand, the Russian administration promised not to let NATO take over. On the other hand, there was a clear threat. NATO had begun carpet bombing of Kosovo.

If we did not accept, the Russians made it clear they would withdraw their support and we would be condemned in the international media as warmongers who wouldn't even accept a peace plan from our Russian brothers. So we agreed to sign. Our government leadership discussed it, and then it was discussed in parliament, which voted to sign the agreement.

After the October 5th coup-d'état I resigned the presidency. I didn't have to do that. We could have mounted a counter attack. But our government discussed the situation. It was our opinion that the foreign powers wanted to provoke a bloodbath. Their idea was, we would strongly resist; their Fifth Column would stage violent provocations; we would act to preserve order; and then their agents would stage murderous incidents for the camera, blaming us to create the impression of ruthless repression. Then under cover of defending themselves they could carry out a Chilean solution, supported by outside forces.

Also, many ordinary people were at that time deceived by the DOS media, by the demonizing of our government and by many false promises, seemingly backed-up by images from Western TV, seductive images of wealth. It was our opinion that NATO wanted to provoke civil war, have a blood bath and let the Serbs kill each other. Create a pretext for intervention. We have direct experience with war. The losses cannot be replaced. So if possible, it is better to make a struggle in the political sphere. So I resigned. This took the Americans by surprise. I am told that [U.S. Secretary of State Madeleine] Albright called Steven Erlanger from the NY Times on the sixth of October, very upset. "Is it possible he resigned?" She couldn't believe it. It spoiled their plans.

Do you think current economic problems stem from the incompetence of the new authorities, or have they been deliberately created? The economy has been ruined.

Competent managers have been driven out using violence or

threats. They've been replaced with people who are incompetent but do what the authorities tell them. And what do they tell them? To paralyze the economy and to bankrupt entire industries so they can be sold for peanuts to their patrons in the West. This isn't like old-fashioned colonialism. The foreigners put their proxies in power and simply strip the country, destroy local productive capacity and then dump their junk. In the first winter after the NATO bombing [i.e., the winter of 1999–2000] we had no restrictions on heating. That was a fierce winter. The next winter was mild, but the new so-called Democrats Milosevic is referring to the "Democratic" Opposition of Serbia, which seized power in a coup-d'état Oct. 5, 2000 with all their promises that the West would do this and do that—what did they achieve? Constant electrical shortages, and remember, we heat mostly with electricity.

There is a lot more to the statement, but the salient features have been included here, in which the late President Milosevic gives an excellent account of the methods used by New World Order and makes it plain that the onslaught against Serbia was an integral part of the advancement of the New World Order. His strikingly— clear account of the dishonesty of Clinton, Hollbrooke and Albright and the treasonous conduct of General Wesley Clark make chilling reading, for what we are seeing in print is the actual modus operandi to be used in all future conquests of nation states.

The war on Yugoslavia is the blueprint for wars to be fought, beyond the conspiracy, for and on behalf of the New World Order, in which the United States will continue to play the leading role.

Chapter 10

Dictatorships Seldom Appear to Start as Such

Dictatorships often arise as something else and seldom come in the full dress uniform of repressive regalia. Felix Dzerzhinsky used to stride round Moscow looking very much like a Russian peasant from the country with an ill-fitting, old narrow peak-cap jammed on the back of his head. From there he graduated to an older-model Rolls Royce to prowl the streets of Moscow. The nuclei of Stalin's dreaded secret police began evolving in 1905 after the Russo-Japan war. The gruesome Bolsheviks did not just suddenly "arrive" 1917.

When Julius Caesar crossed the Rubicon between civilian and military authority with one Roman legion, the tradition that protected the civilian government from victorious generals flushed with power was breached, and that was the beginning of the radical change from a Roman Republic into a Roman Empire.

The similarities between the events I have just mentioned and the current Bush administration are quite easy to spot, especially with the huge expenditure on the military. Our Founding Fathers warned about having a standing army that would eventually grow to be a threat to our liberty.

Read the words of St. George Tucker:

> Whenever standing armies are kept, the rights of the people, liberty, if not already annihilated, is on the brink of destruction.

In the very first instance, the highest law of the land, the U.S. Constitution, is violated by the presence of the large armed force of U.S. military in Iraq where it has no legal authority to be under the U.S. Constitution or under international law. Fearing that Caesar would become a king and that the rule of law would be compromised (does this sound familiar?), the Senate not approving of the radical changes enacted by Caesar, assassinated him. From the civil wars that followed, Caesar's grand nephew, Octavian, emerged as the first Roman emperor, Caesar Augustus. America's Founding Fathers were learned men. They knew Greek and Roman history and wished to prevent history being repeated in the new young nation.

Even at the beginning of our Republic, constitutional anarchists working in secret set as their goal the destruction of the highest law of the land; the U.S. Constitution and the Bill of Rights. In so doing, they tried to pervert the principle: That the Constitution is the highest law of the land and the Constitution alone in the form in which it was framed is the only way that a fair, honest government will endure. The words of the Hon. Hannis Taylor ought to set in stone and be noted with care and concern:

> *Your petitioner represents that the history of our Constitution, taken as a whole, is made up of a series of efforts to evade it whenever the provisions become inconvenient to the particular class at a particular time.*

Hannis Taylor had petitioned the Senate to stop President Wilson's flagrant abuse of power and violation of his oath in conscripting the militia to fight in WWI, which he was in nowise empowered to do. Were he alive today, Taylor would certainly have petitioned the court again:

> *Our petition presented to the court of the people of the United States represents that never in our history has our nation stood in greater perils than it does today in 2006, due to the willful destruction of the United States Constitution. The rise to power of the Republican War Party and its Supreme Court*

> *appointed leader, magistrate George Bush was rapid and is proving to be an unmitigated disaster for the American nation. The two political parties have joined forces in collusion to roil the Constitution.*

Woodrow Wilson, a Socialist posing as a Democrat was one of the worst of a line of non-constitutionalists who have thus far occupied the White House. He destroyed the tariff system, dragged the U.S. into WWI and set up powers for himself that the executive was never supposed to have. Wilson put the American nation on the road to dictatorship which took only a few decades to evolve into the current reality. And the Republican Party (except for Bob La Follette) largely aided and abetted Wilson in his horrific crimes against the nation, not the least being to open the door to international Socialism.

Hitler allowed the Reichstag fire to happen in order to generate a crisis. Both the judicial and legislative branches of government collapsed, opening the door to rule by fiat. Hitler's decrees became law. The German people agreed to decree by fiat because of the climate of crisis and terror that had been created. The Decree for the Protection of People and State (Feb. 28, 1933) suspended guarantees of personal liberty and permitted arrest and incarceration without trial. The Enabling Act (March 23, 1933) transferred legislative power to Hitler, thereby empowering him to rule by decree laws, (proclamations, now called executive orders) laws moreover that are now in force in the U.S. that deviate from the Constitution, thereby making it of no effect.

The Bolsheviks were ten thousand times worse. They made no pretense of their intentions. Theirs was an open conspiracy to rob Russia of its nation-statehood, and bring it down. Thanks to Britain and the United States, the Bolshevik power-grab through a bloody revolution was successful, and they openly committed the worst atrocities ever seen up to that time, knowing that they had the tacit approval of both the U.S. and Britain. The Bolsheviks revolutionaries seized absolute power, and their power became absolute. It remains one of the best examples of what H. G. Wells called "the open conspiracy."

The U.S. Constitution forbids absolute power. The U.S. Constitution defines absolute power as "arbitrary power." It forbids the exercise of arbitrary power, and condemns so-called "laws " like the Patriot Act; establishing secret courts, and agencies devoted to massive spying on the people. Is the United States today close to the condition of the USSR in 1931? The answer is in the affirmative. The Roman Empire was not based on any ideology. It was based on naked power. And whenever the Roman people become alarmed at this condition, then the army excited wars for their "safety and security," and that kept the populace quiet in the mistaken belief that what the Roman Army was doing was for the good of the citizens of Rome. Surely the conduct of the Bush administration is a perfect overlay of the Roman Empire?

The masters of the French Revolution declared it was based on liberty, fraternity and equality, but it soon evolved into mob rule (democracy) accompanied by institutional violence and rule by fiat. Hitler's dictatorship was largely personal and agenda-based.

The dictatorship that emerged from the Bolshevik Revolution was based in a poor type of ideology; the ideology of a dictatorial government that Lenin declared was the Communist Party's dictatorship over the Russian people. Lenin said: " ... *that rests directly on force, not limited by anything, not restricted by any laws, or any absolute rules.*" Can thinking people in the U.S. today not see the similarity between the Bolsheviks and the heavily infiltrated Republican Party of today? The Communist Party dictatorship ruled by coercion alone, unrestrained by any limitations or inhibitions, using secret courts, secret trials, secret torture, prisons and secret executions, with a massive state apparatus to keep the people in fear and trembling and not daring to question the new reign of terror. Yet Wilson applauded the Bolsheviks and said that "something marvelous (or words to that effect) has happened in Russia."

Wilson could say that because he was a deeply committed Socialist who was put in power to wreck the U.S. Constitution in order to bring Socialism to the United States, a goal every succeeding president has worked to support. Moreover, Wilson in all likelihood saw in Russia a model for a future United States of America.

Like Wilson, Franklin D. Roosevelt was an open Socialist. His rise to power came through the contrived situation he and his cabinet planned to happen at Pearl Harbor. Pearl Harbor did more than destroy lives and property, it gave Roosevelt an *excuse,* a license *to* savage the U.S. *Constitution to* a point where it could not be repaired, and he did that with the complicity—(with a few notable exceptions) of men in the Democrat and Republican parties. Roosevelt merged the separation of powers in his phony declaration of "war on poverty" until today, that cornerstone of the Constitution is so undermined that the whole Constitution is ready to fall.

The merging of powers came *to the fore* with the phony, *bogus* "War Powers Act." We have seen versions of the same bogus "power" being "transferred" to the magistrate since the 1991 invasion of Iraq, by a meek and mild Congress when the Congress knew that it *could do no such thing.* The powers *of* war and peace are vested solely in the Congress, but Roosevelt set to work with his wrecking ball and eventually succeeded in smashing down that barrier. There is no empowerment, expressed or expressly implied, in the U.S. *Constitution that* would allow for the creation of the CIA, the FBI, the NSA, the NRO the ATF; FISA, "Gang of Eight": "Gang of Four": secret courts, secret budgets, closed door meetings, secret prisons, and secret torture chambers.

There is no power in the U.S. Constitution called "Executive Order," because an "executive order" is tantamount to legislating and the Executive branch is absolutely prohibited from legislating.

The magistrate—which is a more correct title than "President"—is there to uphold laws passed by the legislature and nothing else. ALL executive orders are bogus, except those FIRST fully debated by the legislature, passed in to law by the Congress, and then given to the President to announce as an act of Congress, not as an act of the President. There is no power in the U.S. Constitution, expressed, or expressly implied that gives to government powers other than those enumerated in the delegated powers Article I Section 8 Clauses 1–18; and nowhere is the power to make war or peace given to the executive, nor does the government or any branch of it or any of its officers have any power to alter or suspend the Constitution save and except by a constitutional amendment submitted to the states for ratification.

Even then it would not be an "amendment," but would be an act to make a new Constitution. But Roosevelt ignored these restrictions and gave himself "war powers," and the Republicans, with some notable exceptions went right along with the power grab.

Today we have President Bush alleging that he has "war powers granted to him by the Congress" and he has set about establishing agencies that have radically altered the shape of the Constitution and torn up its safeguards. And the Democrats by and large (Senator Joseph Lieberman is a good example of one of them) have gone along with the magistrate in the White House.

Both the Republican and Democrat Parties use the subterfuge of "executive orders" to get around the restriction of the U.S. Constitution.

Both parties, thereby, threaten the 10th Amendment, and by their actions also threaten the very State of the Union, because an executive order is a threat by both parties to dissolve the republican form of government guaranteed by the framers of the Constitution to the several States and codified in the 10th Amendment to the U.S. Constitution.

U.S. Constitution—Amendment 10 Powers of the state and people

The powers not delegated to the United States by the Constitution, nor prohibited by it to the states, are reserved to the States respectively, or to the people.

An "executive order" (the same thing as Lenin and Stalin's decrees) destroys that guarantee by destroying the 10th Amendment in fact and in deed making the 10th Amendment of no effect.

Under this direct attack on States rights guaranteed to the States by the Founding Fathers; the States have every right to secede under conditions perpetrated by Congress; —indeed it is their duty to secede from the Union. Roosevelt, the Socialist Democrat dictator was able to pack the Supreme Court and drag the U.S. down to the level of Bolshevik Russia. The Republicans allowed it to happen, again, with a few notable exceptions.

Senator Schell, Congressional Record, Senate:

> *Beginning with Wilson there was a constant fight to drag us down to the level of Europe The same personnel as in Wilson's time, the same wrecking crew that took us into the war and ruined us, is now in command (in Roosevelt's cabinet).*

> *The president's first "noble" experiment when he came into office was to look for some means by which he could find something he was not anywise authorized to do; look for some secret way of slipping something over. His chance came when Florence Kelly presented him with the Fabian Sodalist book, "A New Deal."*

Does all of this not have a very familiar ring to it? What is the difference between Roosevelt's imaginary "war on poverty" created by his attorney general and the bogus "war on terror" imposed on the American people by King George Bush, Prince Richard Cheney and ex-Grand Duke Donald Rumsfeld? In short, there is no difference. A fraud was perpetrated on the American people in 1933 and a fraud was perpetrated on the American people for the second time in 2001.

Rupert Murdoch Dr. Howard Perlmutter Congressman McFadden

e Bank Boston

Senator Henry Jackson

Slobodan Milosevic

Madeleine Albright Wesley K. Clark

Victor Yushchenko Eduard Shevardnadze

Micheal Kozak

Wiliam Walker

Carla Del Ponte Yevgeny Primakov

John Jacob Astor Nelson Wilmarth Aldrich August Belmont

Giulio Andreotti Walter H. Annenberg Richard Holbrooke

Curzio Malaparte

Chapter 11

Dissolving the Covenant

I n this first seven years of the 21st century the United States loudly has trumpeted; this is a land of democracy with civil liberty and justice for all. But is it? First of all, our Founding Fathers said they would have no dealings with a democracy so they established the United States as a Republic.

One of the chief detractors among the delegates to the Convention, Governor Randolph of Virginia expressed his disquiet about democracy:

> *Our chief danger arises from the democratic parts of our constitutions... None of the constitutions have provided sufficient checks against democracy... The evils we experience flow from the excess of Democracy ... the people were not lacking in virtue, but were the dupes of pretended patriots.*

A closer look at the massive Echelon spy system being utilized by an unconstitutional organization, the National Security Agency (NSA) to spy on American citizens in a manner far exceeding anything ever done by Lenin and Stalin, quickly brings the realization that the United States has in fact created an actual incipient dictatorship. And the horror of it is that the Democrats and the Republicans have gone along with it without a murmur of protest. Does ideology play a role in the emerging U.S. dictatorship? Categorically, it does not. The demise of U.S. Republic is largely traceable of historical developments. Lincoln was the first American dictator. That sounds harsh, but there is solid evidence to back it. Lincoln justified his dictatorship in the name of preserving the Union. His extra-legal, extra-constitutional methods (like suspending habeas corpus and imposing martial law), were tolerated in order to suppress Northern opposition to Lincoln's war against the Southern secession, which act of secession was lawful and constitutional.

The Southern States had every right and indeed a duty to secede from the Union as Lincoln had violated the 10th Amendment that guaranteed a Republican form of government to them at the time of the Union. And Lincoln lied when characterized the secession attempt as a rebellion. This enabled him to call out the militia and "suspend" habeas corpus. Do we not see an echo in this in the lies told about Iraq's non-existent "Weapons of Mass Destruction" and the mass of arbitrary laws piled one atop the other, all of which have torn away every vestige of protection once afforded by the U.S. Constitution? If we cannot see this, then God help the American people.

The first major attack on the U.S. Constitution after Lincoln came with magistrate Wilson taking ten powers he was not entitled to take. Here again, the Republicans allowed him to get away with it and even backed his declaration of war against Germany when more than 87% of the American people were against it such as war.

The attack on the separation of powers, which is the cornerstone for our political system, came with the response of the Roosevelt administration to the crisis of the Great Depression. The "New Deal" (taken from a Fabian Socialist book of the same title as shown in my book, One *World Order Socialist Dictatorship*) resulted in Congress delegating its legislative powers to the executive branch, in total abrogation of the Constitution. Today when Congress rubber stamps a statute it is little more than an authorization for an agency of the executive branch to make the law by writing the regulations that are then implemented by bogus proclamations, so-called "executive orders."

All laws have to be explicit, tightly written and clearly defined. Up to the advent of the *New Deal*, legislation was tightly written to prevent judges inserting their predilections between the lines of the Constitution, and this was embodied in the 9th Amendment to the U.S. Constitution, which is a restriction on presidents and or judges expressing their own ideas as if they were in the Constitution. That is to say, no "understanding" by the executive leading to alteration was tolerated, and rightly so, and there is no such unlawful "signing statements" to be found in the Constitution.

The executive branch is there to uphold the law, not interpret it. The National Security Agency (NSA) is a dangerous example of what happens when the 10th Amendment is flouted.

This is not the way a Republic is supposed to be run. By "allowing" executive orders to become law, the law is no longer accountable to the people. If the magistrate who enforces the law also writes the law, then a mockery is made of "all legislative powers being vested in elected representatives in Congress."

The people, the sovereigns, are then disenfranchised, their Constitution is violated; and the separation of powers is breached. Is this not a cause for States who are violated by so-called "executive orders" to secede from the Union? There is no doubt this is the case.

I represent that it is a prime cause for seceding from the Union. The principle that power delegated to Congress by the people cannot be delegated by Congress to the executive branch is the sheet anchor of the U.S. Republic and its Constitution.

Until Presidents Lincoln overturned this principle the executive branch was given absolutely no role in interpreting the law and in setting up its own agencies to enforce that interprétation. That is exactly what the Roman Empire was based on and why it collapsed. The United States will go the same way unless this rot is swiftly halted.

Justice John Marshall Harlan wrote:

> *That congress cannot delegate legislative power to the president is a principle universally recognized as vital to the integrity and maintenance of the system of government ordained by the Constitution.*

Seven decades of an imperial presidency that was ordained to be no more than a mere magistracy begun with Socialist President Wilson breaching the separation of powers, has destroyed that integrity, until today the Republican War Party and its attorneys continue to write "opinions" for an imperial President, bent on concentrating more power in the executive, no matter how blatantly unconstitutional it is. They are the ones who told the magistrate to constantly refer to himself as "the commander in chief," to create non-existent powers for himself,—and the Congress let the rot continue without any attempts to check it. NSA is the outcome of an imperial presidency much as it was the outcome of the transformed Roman Empire under Caesar. The determined drive to enlarge the President's powers predates the Bush administration, and it is being fed to a dangerous degree in the second term of President G. W. Bush current in the year 2007.

The confirmation of Bush' nominee, Samuel Alito, a member of the Federalist Society, to the Supreme Court, and a confirmed believer in merging of powers in favor of the magistrate at the expense of Congress, will provide five votes in favor of a dangerously-enlarged presidential power grab that will lead to a full-blown dictatorship being established in the U.S.

President Bush has used "signing statements" hundreds of times to amend the meaning of statutes passed by Congress. Where this power has come from is clear. It arose out of the prostitution of the Constitution that began with Lincoln, was expanded under

Wilson and then further prostituted under Roosevelt.

For example, Bush has asserted that he has the power to ignore the McCain amendment against torture, to ignore the law that requires a warrant to spy on Americans, to ignore the prohibition against indefinite detention without charges or trial; and to ignore the Geneva Conventions to which the U.S. is signatory. He also claims that he can declare war and domestic spying in pursuance of that war. Bush is asserting the powers that were seized by Wilson.

His Federalist Society apologists and Department of Justice appointees claim that President Bush has the same power to interpret the Constitution as the Supreme Court. Where do they get this from? Certainly not from the U.S. Constitution which clearly spells out, that the office of the executive is no more than a mere magistrate to uphold the laws passed by the legislature. General Lee once said that the president was nothing more than a magistrate who had to carry out the orders of the Congress. There is no equality here between the President and the Congress.

An Alito Court is likely to give its assent to such baseless and false claims. There is no greater danger to the Republic of the United States than this issue, not even the mess we created in Iraq. It is the most crucial issue before the people, perhaps on the same level of crisis as the Civil War. But the people are in shell shock, thanks to the Tavistock Institute and the jackals of the media, relegated Alto's role to the background through the subterfuges of political battles over abortion and homosexual rights.

Many people support Bush—and this is particularly true of the Christian right—because they believe they are fighting against legitimizing sodomy and murder in the womb, and that in supporting President Bush who they perceive as standing up to the Muslim world and the "Liberals," they are "doing the right thing." How sadly mistaken they will find themselves when they wake up in the New World Order-One World Government.

The majority of the American people are unaware that the real issue is not the so-called "war on terror " (which is as much of a fraud as Roosevelt's "war on poverty"), but the war against the evil men who have as their objective the destruction of the Constitution because it stands athwart their plans for a New World Order.

The majority of the American people are completely unaware that these men are on the verge of elevating the executive above the legislature and the courts. Their President would be above the law. Bush Justice Department official and Berkeley law professor John Yoo argues that no laws can restrict the President in his role as commander-in-chief. Thus, once at war (which we are not)—and they are declaring the miasma in Iraq as an "open-ended war on terror" (notwithstanding that open-ended war is outlawed by the Constitution since no war can be funded for more than two years) it is their contention that Bush cannot have any checks and balances placed upon him as "commander in chief." I say John Yoo is out of his depth and does not know the Constitution. Bush's Justice Department says the President is free to undertake any action in pursuit of war, including torture, indefinite spying, and detention of American citizens without judicial restraints "interfering" with his decisions.

The commander-in-chief is a role sufficiently "broad to expand to any crisis," whether it is genuine or contrived. The fact that the Justice Department and its Federalist lawyers are 100% wrong and that the President is not and cannot be the commander chief in peacetime (the current status of the country) and thus the title cannot be conferred upon him and, even it was conferred after a declaration of war, the President still has no war powers, makes little difference to them. Thus there can be little doubt that the U.S. has arrived at the brink of an incipient dictatorship. It is unlikely the developing constitutional crisis—possibly the start of the Second American Revolution—has sunk through to the awareness level of the American people who have thus far failed to recognize that the Constitution is being trampled and roiled as never before in its history and that it is on the verge of being relegated to status of the dead Magna Carta.

America's gradual descent into dictatorship is the result of historical developments that began with Lincoln and gained impetus through a series of presidents that brought forth bitter conflict, even the of old political battles dating back to the Civil War. The so-called "constitutional crisis " that arose when President Nixon was forced out of office by a Democratic Congress is but a pale shadow of the current constitutional crisis. The main difference is that the jackals of the media, whose nightly howls in the night sky over Washington D.C. played such a crucial role in Watergate, are now strangely silent, while they watch the Constitution being put through a meat grinder.

As we come to the close of the last quarter of 2007, there are no constitutional parties. Both political parties, most constitutional lawyers, and the bar associations have abandoned the Constitution and willingly make it of no effect whenever it interferes with their unconstitutional agendas. Americans have forgotten the Founding Fathers and the generation that followed; they have forgotten the blood and sacrifice of our noble forbears in their great struggle for liberty and justice for all. The American people are at the very threshold to losing their constitutional system and civil liberties—permanently. The New World Order will become a reality unless the Constitution is restored to its rightful place and that means getting rid of domestic spying through or by any other means, prohibiting all domestic activities by the CIA the NSA and FISA. It also means scrapping the Homeland Security Act, the Patriot Act, the Driver License Act, drastically curtailing the executive and returning it to its proper function, that of a magistrate to defend the laws of the Union. The 2nd, 4th, 5th, and 10th Amendments must be elevated to their pre-eminent role and the country must once again become a nation of laws and not of men.

Unless this can be brought about, the United States as envisaged by our Founding Fathers and the generation that followed is doomed to destruction. If we are to prevent such a terrible disaster from coming upon us, We, the People, the sovereign owners of the U.S. Constitution must send delegations to the House and Senate from each of the 50 sovereign, independent nations that make up the United States and we must demand from our representatives that they return the U.S. to constitutional government.

If they will not, then they must be forced from office using the remedies laid out in the sovereign people's Constitution. We must have the delegates demand that the words of Rep. Denison contained in the Congressional Globe, January 31, 1866, pages 546–549 be implemented forthwith, brooking no delay:

> *And so it was competent for the States when they created this government organization and called it the United States, by the Constitution to delegate therein certain powers and the right to do certain things, and thus place the powers delegated under the control of the Federal majorities and reserve certain powers to be controlled by the people of each State, and for the exercise and control of they were not answerable to any other power.*
>
> *If the States did absolutely and unconditionally reserve these powers, then they cannot be taken away from them by two thirds of this House and three-quarters of the States anymore than the majority of stockholders in a bank in which I might have stock, can take over my horse, or my farm for use of the corporation, because the States never placed these reserved powers in the common fund of powers controlled by the Federal majorities.*
>
> *Their conditions were the same as to these reserved powers after adoption of the Constitution as before. The people of each State constituted sovereignty before the adoption of that instrument. They were equally sovereign over the reserved rights after its adoption and they cannot be taken away, except by the will of each State, unless there is to be*

something in the Constitution to authorize it; for a State, like an individual, cannot be bound further than it agrees to bind itself.

Have the States parted with these rights by agreeing to amend the Constitution? If so, then these powers were not reserved absolutely, but only retained until the Federal majorities as represented by two-thirds of the House and three-fourths of the States may choose to transfer them against the will of the people of the State, or it may be one-fourth of the State, or three-fourths of-fourths of the States from the States may choose to transfer them against the will of the people of the State. Or it may be one—fourth of the States, from the respective States, to the Federal Government. This point ought to be settled by the Constitution and I think it is…

The most important feature of the 10th Amendment is that it fixes the limitations of the Federal Government which is one of delegated powers and not original powers. It makes it impossible for government to take any power by inference.

The power to be taken or exercised must be must be clearly expressed in the Constitution or it cannot be taken. In Article 5 there is the right to amend, but not to make new. It would not be an amendment to abolish the Constitution and adopt the Communist Manifesto of 1818, or the laws of France.

An amendment has to be something germane to the instrument, it must be something already in the Constitution, or it fails the test of an amendment. But making a new Constitution would only be binding on those States as agree to be bound by it and it could not be become a part of the Constitution until every State adopts it.

(Excerpted from What You Should Know About The U.S. Constitution, Revised and Updated 2007 Edition).

You are urged to read this vital message over and over again until you are familiar with every word, every line of it, for in this message is contained a clear warning that the Bush administration has been and is attempting to make a new

Constitution without consulting the States through a national referendum; which new Constitution would have to be agreed to by all 50 States.

Those who do not agree to a new Constitution are not bound it and are duty bound to secede from the dissolved former Union. Indeed it is their bounden duty as sovereign states to take the necessary action to secede once the Federal Government breaks the original Covenant, which the Bush administration with the connivance of Congress, has done already. We represent the following actions as proof that the Bush administration has already broken the covenant established as the highest law of the land and is therefore guilty of lawless behavior.

As further evidence thereof, we point to the exercise of arbitrary power forbidden by the U.S. Constitution with passage of the following unconstitutional acts:

➤ The invasion and military attack on Iraq without a declaration of war.
➤ Congress purporting to "give" or "grant" the President "permission" or "authorization" to attack Iraq without just cause and without any provision in the U.S. Constitution sanctioning such an attack, in itself a gross violation of the U.S. Constitution.
➤ There being no such power to "give" or "grant" the President War power expressly forbidden to the executive by the U.S. Constitution, the Congress acted in flagrant violation of the highest law of the land and ought therefore to be dismissed forthwith.
➤ Congress and the President have connived and colluded together to violate the separation of powers and the President has taken powers to which he is not entitled, but which powers are expressly forbidden to him.
➤ Assuming the title of commander in chief when Congress has not bestowed the temporary title on him and by assuming powers that totally violate the 10th Amendment to the U.S. Constitution.

- By sending the militia to fight in a foreign war.
- By passage of the unconstitutional Patriot Act and Homeland Security Act both of which grossly violate the 10th Amendment and nullify the 10th Amendment.
- By "making a new Constitution" through adoption of unconstitutional laws without putting such measures to the States for their assent in the manner provided by the U.S. Constitution.
- By spying on the American people in violation of the Fourth Amendment.

These are but a very few of the many acts of dissolution of the U.S. Constitution carried out by the Bush administration with the connivance collusion and consent of both political parties. Therefore I submit that it is the right of the States who so choose, to secede from the Union unless these illegal actions are immediately nullified by the Congress.

In the absence of such action of nullification by the Congress, the people must assemble their own attorneys general and assemble their own grand juries. These grand juries of each state must return indictments against the executive and the Congress for each and every violation of the U.S. Constitution.

The people of the States must then send their representatives to Washington to inform the Federal Government of their actions and to demand that remedial action be taken immediately. If such remedial action is not immediately forthcoming then the sovereign people of the sovereign States must recall their representatives from the House and Senate thus rendering the House and Senate inoperable. We trust that there are men among us of the caliber of Patrick Henry, St. George Tucker, Thomas Jefferson and Henry Clay, men who have the means and the courage to take action to prevent the United States being turned into a virtual dictatorship.

The 1991 invasion of Iraq and the second invasion of Iraq were both outside the pale and the ken of the U.S. Constitution and as such cannot be recognized as lawful. On this one single ground alone, the Congress has the right to order the U.S. military to return to the U.S. together with all of its equipment within 45 days of the announcement by a joint session of the House and Senate. The measures to return constitutional government to We, the People, are in conformity with the precepts and principles of the U.S. Constitution as the lawful remedies available to the sovereign people of the sovereign states.

The alternative is to do nothing about the lawless war raging in Iraq and then watch the transformation from a confederated Republic to a dictatorship take place before our very eyes. And this is only possible through the full cooperation of a compliant media that supports the government all of the way, in other words, a transformation to an open conspiracy as the following shows.

The Press: An Engine of Conformity

The matter of press control (print and electronic) is beyond the conspiracy stage and is right out in the open. Some Americans are still deceived in that they have been led to believe that the Public Broadcasting System (PBS) is independent and the only remaining source of truth and enlightenment. That is unhappily, not the case.

This was brought out by a recent report that Kenneth Y. Tomlinson, chairman of the Corporation for Public Broadcasting (CPB), had on his own initiative without his Board's approval, appointed two ombudsmen to review the content of National Public Radio (NPR) and Public Broadcasting Service (PBS) to correct what in his opinion is blatantly liberal bias.

Ombudsmen Ken Bode (a fellow at the so-called conservative Hudson Institute and from 1998 to 2002, Dean of the Medill School of Journalism at Northwestern University) and William

Schulz (retired from the Readers Digest, where Tomlinson spent most of his working time) are allegedly dedicated to the pursuit of objectivity, but the truth is they would not recognize objectivity if it hit them in the face.

The trusting American public, desperate to find "truth" on public television have long been told that that "this program was made possible, in part, by funding from viewers/listeners like you," while at the same time they are hounded by inescapable begging appeals launched by individual radio and broadcast stations inviting them to "become members" by making donations. Usually, a good half-hour of any broadcast is devoted to such an appeal, and sometimes it runs longer.

Is such a tactic really necessary? Why should PBS be begging for donations when the fact is that such memberships represent only 26% of the total budget spent by CPB? Businesses and charitable foundations make up a combined total of 22.8%, with the Federal government following a distant third with a mere 15.3%. What is wrong with this picture?

In the first instance, individual donors have no organized voice whatsoever in determining or controlling the content of programming. Complaints of bias from right-wing foundations and the telecommunications industry have stifled the Federal government, which chooses the governing board—a board which quite naturally reflects the wishes of the biggest donors and carry the most weight. The current Board of CPB is composed of five Republicans, two Democrats and one "independent."

As already mentioned chairman Kenneth Tomlinson spent much of his career until 1996 at Readers Digest, still after all these years a favorite of Americans who don't have the time to read articles in full. "Conservative" William F. Buckley's National Review's praise of Tomlinson says it all:

Many consider him the magazine's last great editor... Most of the magazine's top editors had been hired by Tomlinson, and virtually all of them were, like Tomlinson himself, political conservatives.

These were people who, apparently, were in line with the thinking of Newt Gingrich, who declared:

I don't understand why they call it public broadcasting. As far as I am concerned, there's nothing public about it; it's an elitist enterprise. Rush Limbaugh is public broadcasting.

(This overlooks the fact that Limbaugh was picked up and given status by Republican wealthy elitist who want their points of view put over).

Tomlinson's view of the media's role comes from his career at the Voice of America (VOA)—set up for propaganda purposes in 1942 during World War II, and reorganized in 1953 as a branch of the U.S. Information Agency, a more discreet title.

A shakeup in 1998 transferred VOA to the Broadcasting Board of Governors (BBG). Kenneth Tomlinson is today chairman both of the BBG and of the CPB and no doubt giving the American public to the same style of propaganda prepared for the "the enemy." Although I have no way to prove it, experience leads me to believe that the Tavistock Institute may have been the guiding light in these changes. Tavistock has a large portfolio of American government and private business accounts in its portfolio.

Tomlinson spoke in late April of 2005 before a Senate Subcommittee on International Operations and Terrorism might well have been "ghost" written for him by the late Edward Bernays or even Beatrice Webb:

Through its adherence to Western journalistic standards, through its objective, accurate reporting, Alhurra [which means "the free one"—a new Arabic-language television network subsidiary of BBC] can gain the credibility we need to build an audience and offer Middle Eastern audiences a new balanced view of world events. While criticism in the Arab press continues, we are connecting with the people— our target audience—and they are sending us hundreds of e-mails to welcome us. "You are much needed to balance biased news controlled by those full of hatred to western world," reads one. "This is the first step to fight the 'hate culture' that feeds terrorism," says another. "I hope your channel [will help] our Arab brothers ... to tell the truth from all that is going on."

However, it is doubtful whether Alhurra can compete with Al Jazeera. How will all these "unbiased" truths be disseminated? In March of 2005 the job of conducting public broadcasting's switch from analog to digital was given to Ken Ferree, the current president and CEO of CPB. After a four-year stint four under FCC chairman Michael Powell, the two share a belief that "strict media ownership limits are outdated in an era of 200 cable channels and the Internet"—Ferree, a lawyer by trade (or profession) applied his legal expertise gained at Goldberg, Wiener and Wright to formulate new rules on media ownership and licensing. Prior to June 2001 Goldberg, Wiener & Wright, represented the privately-held and funded satellite company PanAmSat founded by Greenwich, Connecticut resident, Rene Anselmo.

Anselmo's company was the first and (the biggest) international satellite network, and worked closely with the Hughes Space and Communications Company (founded by Howard Hughes in 1961), a subsidiary of Hughes Electronics, which constructed, launched and maintained PanAmSat's communications satellites.

Ferree represented PanAmSat in its anti-trust claim against COMSAT, the U.S. member of the international consortium called "IntelSat," which at that time had a monopoly on satellite communications based on a treaty. As a direct result of that lawsuit, IntelSat's monopoly was broken to allow PanAmSat to climb to the number-one spot in the digital communications industry.

Following the death of Howard Hughes' in 1976, his medical foundation he had created to own Hughes Aircraft Company as a tax-free trust, was ordered by a U.S. Federal Court to sell off the corporation in 1985 because of its close ties to Hughes Aircraft and its extremely small charitable donations. In the bidding war Ford and Boeing were outbid to acquire the company by General Motors and its chairman stated: "Electronics, we believe, is going to be the key to the 21st Century." Foresight indeed? What was not generally known at that time outside of the defense procurement agencies was that Hughes was manufacturing products such as microchips, lasers and communications satellites—in addition to air-to-air missiles. It was the largest supplier of electronic equipment to the military and the seventh biggest defense contractor.

Probably not known by the public who are customers of Direct TV is that in 1994 Hughes launched its own satellites (licensed as DirecTV) to "compete" with PanAmSat. Only two years later Hughes took over its competitor by acquiring 81% of PanAmSat stock, thus giving Hughes (and its parent GM) control of all American satellite transmission with the exception of a small share of the market held by Echostar.

Thus by this expedient it is possible to control what a very substantial number of Americans will see, and is a valuable tool in opinion-making. Outside the U.S. another satellite tycoon circling the American satellite laager was Rupert Murdoch, the Australian who first founded Sky satellite television network in 1989, and who a year later bought out rival British Satellite Broadcasting to become British Sky Broadcasting.

In 1985, the same year General Motors acquired Hughes, Murdoch purchased seven independent television stations in the

United States and Twentieth Century Fox Holdings. That combination resulted in the creation of the first new television network since the mid-1950s. Murdock then expanded his Australian newspaper chain into Great Britain with his purchase of London's *The News of the World* in 1968 and soon thereafter *The Sun.*

In 1976 he bought the *London Times*—putting all of them under News Corp., created in 1980. Murdoch, a high-level representative of the Committee of 300 had secured a virtual monopoly on what millions of Americans and Britons would see on their televisions screens, and read in the newspapers. Now it was possible to engage in long-range penetration and inner conditioning of millions of people, and literally "brainwash" them.

A silent coup-d'état had taken place without the British and American people ever becoming aware of what was transpiring. In 1988 News Corp. acquired Triangle Publications (including TV Guide) from Walter Annenberg, a crony of Richard Nixon's and whom he had appointed as U.S. Ambassador to Great Britain in 1969. By 1993, Murdoch's influence had made inroads in Asia, when he acquired controlling interest in Asia's Star-TV.

But it was the American satellite market which was Murdoch's prime concern. In order to reduce debt, News Corp. sold 18.6% of the *Fox Entertainment Network,* raising $2.8 billion in 1998, and another $2.9 billion in cash in 2001 by selling *Fox Family Worldwide,* Inc. to Disney. Loaded with cash, Murdoch was ready to take over Hughes's *DirecTV.*

Without waiting for FCC approval (perhaps it had already been given in secret through proxies) EchoStar's offer to purchase *DirecTV* was accepted in October 2001. After a protest staged outside the Justice Department in July 2002 by a "group of Christian broadcasters," the FCC finally announced that it was rejecting the proposed merger to prevent a monopoly harmful to consumers.

An FCC decision issued at the same time allowed Murdoch's News Corp. to acquire 34% of Hughes—resulting in Murdoch's naming himself chairman of Hughes—was overturned on appeal a year later by the Third Circuit of Appeals, which sent the rules back to the FCC to justify its changes. Murdoch has nevertheless proceeded with his satellite television programming while cashing in on the sale of PanAmSat to private equity firm Kohlberg Kravis Roberts & Company (KKR), which then unloaded 27% stakes in the communications satellites to Providence Equity Partners and the Carlyle Group, retaining 44% for itself. Together these shareholders took their stock public in March of 2005—tripling the return on their initial investment—while retaining 55% of the voting shares. The Carlyle Group, as most of us know, is one of the stars in the portfolios of the Committee of 300.

When we analyze the details of ownership, a pattern begins to emerge. There can be no doubt that the stage had been set that went well beyond the conspiracy to an open conspiracy as envisaged by H. G. Wells.

In the meantime, KKR and the Carlyle Group (both with close connections to the Bush family) all very high-level functionaries of the Committee of 300, have seized control of our television viewing. The steps taken by the Committee of 300 are clear. In my opinion President Ronald Reagan gave Murdoch preferential treatment by permitting him to enter the FFC, strictly controlled American market. The Museum of Broadcast Communications website has a very interesting posting—or at least it did have the last time I checked it:

> *His FOX television network was able to avoid complying with the FCC's Financial Interest and Syndication (FinSyn) rules, first, by airing fewer hours of programming than was required to define FOX as a "network" and later, by receiving a temporary FCC waiver of the rules—an action*

the other three broadcast networks vigorously opposed.

Also, Murdoch was the concentrated target of a 1988 effort by Senator Edward Kennedy (no friend of the Committee of 300 since the murder of his brother, the late President John F. Kennedy (and at the time, a frequent target of Murdoch's Boston Herald newspaper to revoke another FCC waiver, one that waived cross-ownership restrictions that would have prevented Murdoch from owning both newspapers and television stations in New York and Boston. The end result of Kennedy's sustained efforts was that Murdoch eventually sold the New York Post (he later would receive a new waiver that allowed him to reacquire the struggling paper in 1993) and put Boston's WFXT-TV into an independent trust.

After selling *The Daily Racing Form*, Annenberg's family became wealthy and "respectable," at Hearst Newspapers. The son of Moe Annenberg, Walter, who, as circulation manager for the Hearst papers, had sought the "advice" of Charles "Lucky" Luciano and Meyer Lansky to help "oversee" the circulation of the *New York Daily Mirror*. It is doubtful whether Walter ever inquired into what methods the two men used.

In 1926, Annenberg left Hearst in order to work full-time on his *Racing Form*, which he had promoted while at the Hearst papers. In 1927 he bought controlling interest in Mont Tennes General News Bureau, known as the race wire service, from a man who was being intimidated by Al Capone. By 1929 Annenberg had made a deal with the Chicago mob that put him in business with Meyer Lansky, Frank Costello and Johnny Torrio. Annenberg then set up a new company called the Universal Publishing Company, which published "wall sheets" and "hard cards." The wall sheets listed races, horses, jockeys, morning odds, and other information that bettors used in deciding how to place their money.

A few years later, Annenberg established Nationwide News Service in Chicago on August 27, 1934 and raised a furor with the Capone mob. As a result, Annenberg to fled to seek the protection of Meyer Lansky who living in Florida at the time. Lansky arranged for Annenberg to transfer his wire service to southern Florida and got a piece of the action in return for keeping Annenberg from getting shot.

For a while the service also operated out of Paradise Island in the Bahamas where Lansky ran a front company called the Mary Carter Paint Company. In 1936, Lansky mended fences with the Mob and allowed Annenberg to reach an agreement with the Capone Syndicate. Good authority has it that Annenberg paid one million dollars a year for protection and was free to pursue other interests without being stalked by paid gunmen.

With the race wire service problem cleared up, Annenberg purchased a newspaper that he felt had the "prestige and class" (something Lansky was always talking about, but which his other ventures lacked)—*the Philadelphia Inquirer.* Annenberg had learned a great deal since 1934, and achieved great success in increasing the overall circulation of the Inquirer. He took great care to shape it to become a successful tool and model for Republican Party politics and a vehicle for promoting the New World Order, albeit very subtly.

The contacts his son Walter made with the Republicans resulted in his being named Ambassador to Great Britain by President Richard Nixon. Upon Walter Annenberg's death in 1994, naturally, his obituary failed to mention such trifling details, because he had donated a small percentage of his gain from vice to charity.

Let no one be in doubt that we are controlled by the media just as the media itself is controlled. This is a conspiracy fact, not speculation, and the situation is now quite out in the open. No doubt this system would be very difficult to sustain were it not for the secret funding of the various U.S. sponsored and favored projects, which I bring out into the open, beyond the conspiracy.

Chapter 12

The Secret Off-Budget U.S. Spending Program Unlocked

The Federal Reserve Act is what has made these aforementioned acts so significant is the control it gives to the Committee of 300 over the American people. It also made possible the unlawful wars in Iraq, on the basis that the United States government has operated a secret "off-budget" and spending program for decades in defiance of the highest law of the land, the U.S. Constitution. The institutional and political foundation of this system of secret finances dates back to the opium trade with China and later Turkey of the 18th and 19th century.

Its vehicle was the British East India Company (BEIC) a closed corporation with a royal charter. At the end of the 19th and 20th centuries, the consolidation of American industry and banking was firmly under the control of corporations that had taken over the economy, particularly the Military Industrial Complex. The great fascist leaders of American industry and finance in the late nineteenth century were superb practitioners of covert operations; based on experience gained from their business in the opium trade with China. The institutions they established during the nineteenth and twentieth centuries have remained unchanged and are the same institutions through which their descendants maintain control to this very day.

This is a summary of the structure of the American political economy, which fits the facts better than the official model. Officially, American capitalism is characterized by democracy, opportunity, self-improvement, open and free markets, and constructive regulation for the public good, in short, happiness, or the pursuit of happiness as stated in the U.S. Constitution. In this model leaders have the nation's interests at heart, and politicians attend to their constituencies. Unhappily, the truth is very different. Why the United States is so widely misunderstood is due in part to a controlled educational system and media. As the system evolved over the decades, time lent it legitimacy spanning the political spectrum. Once monopoly control had been achieved, the proletariat would rise and its dictatorship would begin. We shy away from such determinism; nothing happens but as a consequence of what men do and choose to do.

At the time of the attack on the World Trade Center and the Pentagon in September 2001 according to the Government Accounting Office (GAO), Pentagon had incurred $3.4 trillion of "non-documented transactions," that is to say that there were $3.4 trillion worth of financial transactions for which there was no discernible purpose. The day before the attack, Secretary of Defense Donald Rumsfeld warned that the lack of control over its budget was a greater danger to the national security of the United States than terrorism. After the attacks, the government stopped publicly disclosing information about "non-documented transactions."

The problem is not restricted to the Pentagon, but affects the entire spectrum of government agencies and departments from the Education Department, the Bureau of Indian Affairs to the Defense Department. For a number of years the GAO has compiled a parallel set of books for the Federal Government called the Financial Report of the United States. This report attempts to impose "Generally Accepted Accounting Principles" to the government's financial reporting process in order to give a clearer picture of the government's actual assets and liabilities and thereby enable better planning. Neither the Pentagon nor the Department of Housing and Urban Development (HUD), to name just two, have ever been able to pass a GAO audit on this basis.

Significantly, the government does not employ double entry bookkeeping in the preparation of its accounts, which has been standard accounting practice since the seventeenth century that classifies and tracks sources and uses of funds to create an accurate picture of a business (or public) enterprise. Running a 21st century military machine using antique accounting methods is an anomalous situation with interesting implications, not least of which is that government agencies cannot, or will not, explain what they are doing with the money that is appropriated for their operations by Congress. A similar state of affairs prevails at the Department of Housing and Urban Development (HUD). It exists primarily, at least in law, to ensure that low income Americans have access to affordable housing, which HUD provides as well as both credit and credit insurance on a nationwide scale. Yet HUD has never compiled information on its activities so that it or anyone else can see, by place, whether or not its activities in that place make money, lose money, or are simply irrelevant.

Few Americans are probably aware that Lockheed Martin, builder of the F22 air superiority fighter, is also a major outside contractor supplying financial control and accounting systems to the Pentagon. The Pentagon for its part is Lockheed Martin's biggest customer. This example is by no means unique. Lockheed also has a subsidiary employed by HUD to administer housing in American cities, an unusual diversification for a corporation the majority of whose business is done with the military and intelligence agencies.

Similarly Dyncorp (recently acquired by Computer Sciences Corporation) is another contractor that, like Lockheed, derives almost all its revenue from government security and military contracts. It is also a contractor supplying information technology to a variety of government agencies including the Pentagon, HUD, the Securities and Exchange Commission (SEC) and the Department of Justice. At the Department of Justice it manages the case management software used by DOJ lawyers to manage investigations.

This is a prime example of an open conspiracy, or to put it another way, it is a situation which goes well beyond a conspiracy. An example of overlapping interests is Herbert "Pug" Winokur. Not only was he on Dyncorp's board of directors, but he was also the Enron director in charge of that company's risk management committee, and a long-standing board member of the Harvard Management Corporation, which invests in HUD projects. AMS Inc., a computer software firm hired by HUD in 1996 to take over the management of its internal software for accounting and financial control, presided in two short years over an explosion in undocumented transactions of nearly $76 billion. AMS violated fiduciary and control practices by installing its own equipment and software with no parallel runs against the legacy software and accounting system.

In those same two years, HUD's management more than tripled the volume of loan and insurance business being pushed through the system. Anyone familiar with running such systems in a bank or an insurance company immediately understands that a decision such as this (for it had to be a decision) would result in huge losses. Is this incompetence or design? Only the credulous would believe incompetence. The reward for Charles Rossotti, president of AMS, was to be named Internal Revenue Service (IRS) Commissioner at the Department of the Treasury, from which position he oversaw significant Treasury contract amendments to AMS. He was a direct beneficiary of this as a special White House waiver permitted Rossotti and his wife to retain their AMS stock.

The reaction of many people to the sorts of facts related above is to dismiss them as no more than evidence of incompetence and accident, not some conspiracy. By this relative openness, the U.S. has now gone beyond the conspiracy into the phase of what Wells called an "open conspiracy."

Firms such as IMB, AMS Lockheed, Dyncorp, SAIC and Accenture have failed to provide systems that can pass a GAO audit. This maneuvering and the government's justifications affront common sense and are unethical. As private sector firms, they have to pass audits before their own accounts can be approved and reported to shareholders. Yet they routinely fail to meet the same standard for the government.

Often the government blames the previous, outgoing administration. However, consider that the incoming Bush administration replaced all the senior Clinton political appointees except the Comptroller of the Currency, John D. Hawke; IRS commissioner Charles Rossotti (formerly of AMS); Comptroller General David Walker (and CIA director George Tenet.

In short, the key positions necessary for the control of the federal credit, financial control, audit and intelligence, so that the Bush administration cannot blame the Clinton administration.

This undisturbed transition from Democratic to Republican administrations represented a remarkable cross-party consensus, and highlights the real positions of power. With the exception of Rossotti, all these men were still in place in 2004. And what of Rossotti? He left the IRS to become a senior adviser to the Carlyle Group for information technology. A more richly symbolic and meaningful job move could scarcely be imagined. Carlyle's business is global venture capital, which is to say it invests in corporate acquisitions all over the world specializing in arms manufacturers and technology. The large levels of non-documented transactions at HUD and the Department of Defense inevitably inspire curiosity. Where is the money associated with those transactions? It is no great leap of imagination to wonder equally where the Carlyle Group raises the money with which to finance its acquisitions.

The cartelization of the American economy was for all intents and purposes completed by the end of the first decade of the twentieth century. In 1889, America's leading banker J.P. Morgan held a meeting at his 5th Avenue mansion in New York. Its purpose was to reach a consensus whereby the owners of America's railroads merged their competing interests. This was no mere group of transportation executives agreeing to fix prices. The railroads also controlled the nation's coalfields and oil supplies and were tightly bound to the nation's largest banks.

The creation of the Federal Reserve in 1914 completed this process of consolidation. In effect, Congress ceded control of the U.S. currency system and the federal credit to the banks, thereby officially recognizing the cartel. This placed a relatively small number of men in a position to set prices across the economy with a degree of control heretofore unknown in the history of the United States.

American foreign policy and the wars that America has fought over the course of the twentieth century (including the Spanish American War in 1898 and the present War on Terror) have successfully extended the cartel's control over the world economy. The American Civil War was fought to determine control of the U.S. economy, and not to abolish slavery. Most Americans would explain the last 150 years of warfare as sadly necessary for reasons beyond America's control. The implication is that America has accumulated its preponderant international position by some providential accident and not by design. Arguments for a contrary view elicit derisive accusations of falling victim to "conspiracy theory." Reassuringly, they believe that self-interested individuals and organizations are incapable of collaboration to achieve common ends.

When J.P. Morgan hammered out a non-compete agreement, it was no accident. Similarly, neither have America's wars been accidents; they have been far more profitable than is widely understood. The U.S. confiscated billions of dollars worth of German and Japanese war treasure at the end of World War Two. President Truman made a conscious decision to not reveal this to the public or repatriate it. Instead, it was used to finance covert operations.

Popular myth has it that the trusts were broken in the first decade of the twentieth century thanks to the crusade of Theodore Roosevelt on behalf of the middle class. Roosevelt certainly used his public stance against "big business" to successfully bid for campaign money from the very businessmen whom he was attacking. This perhaps explains why he subsequently signed legislation repealing criminal penalties for those same businessmen. This is a common trait of "liberal" or "progressive" presidents.

The second Roosevelt, Franklin, is remembered as the champion of the downtrodden, who put an end to the Great Depression. It was he who established the nation's social security system which in reality was (and is) funded by a highly regressive tax on its beneficiaries. Matching contributions from business were allowed to be deducted as a business expense before tax, which simply extended the regressive nature of the program by financing business' share out of foregone tax revenue.

Roosevelt, a superb politician, won a landslide victory on a platform of reform which he adroitly sidestepped and did not fulfill. Instead, he declared a national economic emergency, short— circuiting any constitutional challenge to his power in the court. He promptly defaulted on the gold clause in the government's bond contracts, and established the Exchange Stabilization Fund (ESF) in 1934. Ostensibly meant to promote dollar stability in the foreign exchanges, the fund in practice was and is something quite different. It is exempt from reporting to Congress and is answerable only to the President and Secretary of the Treasury. It is, in short, an undisclosed fund that can tap federal credit.

The Mechanism for Enslavement

JOHN COLEMAN

The establishment of the Exchange Stabilization Fund (ESF) was an extension of the same logic behind the creation of the Federal Reserve in 1914. The latter, the Federal Reserve, was also created in response to a crisis: the crash of 1907. The Wall Street legend credits J.P. Morgan's genius and patriotism with saving the Nation.

In reality, the crash and resulting depression enabled Morgan to destroy his competitors, buy up their assets and in the process revealed to the nation and the world just how powerful the banks and Morgan were. Not all were grateful, and some demanded legislative action to bring the federal credit and national monetary system under public oversight and control.

In a campaign of masterful political legerdemain, the Federal Reserve was created in 1912 by an act of Congress to do just this. The Federal Reserve System is probably the most diabolical imposition of slavery forced on the American people and brought about by a conspiracy between international bankers and their surrogates in the U.S. House and Senate.

But by creating it as a private corporation owned by the banks, Congress effectively ceded to the banks a position even stronger than they had occupied before.

Even today it is not widely understood that the Federal Reserve is a privately held business owned by the very interests that it nominally regulates.

Thus the control of federal credit and the U.S. monetary system and the rich flow of insider information that results from that control are veiled from public view and are privately controlled in secret, which rather explains the Delphic nature of the Fed's chairman.

The extension of secret control was not limited to finance. The National Security Act of 1947 created the Central Intelligence

Agency (CIA) and the National Security Council (NSC) and consolidated control of the three armed services under one roof at the Pentagon. This merely served to extend this principle of secrecy to the field of "national security." Like the Federal Reserve, the CIA was exempted from public disclosure of its budget and was given budgetary control over the entire intelligence community, while the National Security Council was set up as a policy-making body separate from the existing organs of state policy, such as the State Department and the military commands reporting directly to the President.

The CIA Act of 1949 created a budget mechanism that allowed it to spend as much money as it wanted "without regard to the provisions of law and regulations relating to the expenditure of government funds." In short, the CIA has a way to fund anything—legal or illegal—behind the protection of national security law.

Having created the bureaucratic means to conceive and make policy in secret, the next development was to create the means to implement it. The main issue was how to control money flows in the national economy. The government's solution was to assume a commanding position in the credit markets.

To that end, it created first the Federal Housing Authority in 1934 (forerunner of HUD and now part of HUD) and subsequently Ginnie Mae and then Fannie Mae and Freddie Mac, which are Government Sponsored Enterprises (GSE's) to supply mortgage finance and insurance for homebuyers. The underlying political purpose is more subtle. Combined with the power of the Federal Reserve (i.e. the cartel) to set the price of money, the ESF, the GSE's and latterly the Department of Housing and Urban Development (HUD) have proven to be a powerful force for regulating money flows and demand in the US economy.

The military, too, was reformed with the adoption for the first time in American history of a wartime military-budget and force structure in peacetime. In the early '60s this was fine tuned with the adoption of an explicit cost-plus acquisition process. The justification for this was, as usual, national security. This military budget has proven as effective in regulating the industrial sector as control over home finance has proven in regulating credit. Together they confer virtual control over the economy as conventionally measured in terms of money Gross Domestic Product) GDP. A few moments reflection on the institutional structure briefly outlined above makes clear the central importance of the federal credit in underwriting it. The federal government underwrites the GSE's by extending to them a subsidized line of credit from the Treasury. An additional indirect subsidy in the form of lower borrowing costs flows from the belief in the marketplace that this constitutes an implicit government guarantee of their solvency.

While this subject from time to time excites controversy, the truth is that the GSE's are not the only corporate entities benefiting from government support.

Since the failure of Continental Illinois in the early 1980's, the government has informally made it clear that it stands behind the banking system. This was made even more explicit with the bailout of Citibank in the early 1990s and the implicit subsidy that the entire banking industry received as a result. Nor are financial institutions the only ones to enjoy this kind of support. Both Lockheed Martin and Chrysler have been effectively saved from insolvency by the taxpayer in the past, presumably due to

their status as major defense contractors. Such a system places a significant value premium on sheer size, if for no other reason than what the banking system cheerfully and disingenuously refers to as the "too-big-to-fail" doctrine. But for industrial firms, too, there is significant value in having a contracting relationship with the Pentagon. Not only is there the economic "nirvana" of cost-plus contracting, but, if you are big enough, your fundamental business risk is underwritten for national security reasons. Thus, there is a tendency for firms to migrate their businesses to military rather than purely civilian markets; today the Boeing Company is a perfect case study of this in action. And a result is that civilian business in sector after sector has been driven into insolvency or into acquisition by the very entities who are supposed to be protecting them.

The dynamics of cost-plus contracting are such that profits rise as costs rise. This explains a great deal about the size of American military budgets, which have risen inexorably over the years even as military preparedness has fallen. But as we have seen, the losses in terms of lower productivity are felt across wide swaths of the economy as non-military contracting competition is squeezed out or acquired.

Obviously these losses in the real economy have to be financed, producing a higher demand for credit than would otherwise be the case. Given declining productivity and a narrowing production base, it was inevitable that at some point net exports would become negative, a condition that the U.S. entered in 1982 and which has intensified since. Currently the US net foreign debt is on the order of $3,000 billion (30% of GDP) and is increasing at a rate of some $500 billion per year (5% of GDP).

To finance such a large foreign borrowing requirement without currency depreciation requires both the ability to control as much of the national cash flow as possible as well as the collaboration of at least a few key foreign countries to achieve the same sort of control over international cash flows. In the latter case, this takes the form, in part, of ever larger amounts of intervention on the part of those countries running dollar surpluses and strong net export positions to prevent the markets from driving the dollar lower.

In practice this means that they accumulate more and more dollars, which they in turn invest in U.S. Treasury securities. Foreigners now own some 45% of U.S. Treasury debt outstanding. In January the Bank of Japan intervened in the currency markets on behalf of Japan's Ministry of Finance, purchasing a whopping $69 billion in that month alone, or more than 30% of its total intervention in 2003, which was itself a record year.

All of this may seem to have little to do with the black budget, which most people associate with intelligence covert "black" operations. The truth, however, is that the black budget cannot be understood in isolation without understanding the political, historical and economic context from which it springs. One way of understanding this is by comparing trends. For example, in 1950 the Dow Jones Industrials stood at 200, and today the Dow is at 10,600. In 1950 narcotics trafficking was a relatively unknown crime in the United States. Today it is endemic, and not only in cities but in smaller towns and rural communities as well. In 1950 the U.S. possessed most of the world's gold and was the world's biggest creditor. Today it is the world's biggest debtor. In 1950 the U.S. was a major exporter of industrial goods to the rest of the world. On current trends the U.S. is not self-sufficient in manufactured goods and will not even have a manufacturing industry worth the name by 2020.

Is there a connection between these trends or are they random? It may seem strange to think of a positive correlation between narcotics trafficking and the stock market, but consider: in the late 1990s the U.S. Department of Justice estimated that the proceeds of such trade entering the U.S. banking system was between $500 and $1,000 billion annually, or more than 5–10% of GDP. The proceeds of crime need to find a way into legitimate, that is legal, channels or they are worthless to the holders. If one further imagines that the banking system earns a fee of 1% for handling this flow (rather low considering that money laundering is a seller's market) then the profits for the banks from this activity are on the order of $5 to $10 billion.

One reason for the Federal Reserve silence is that agencies of the government itself have been involved in drug trafficking for more than sixty years. For the purposes of understanding the black budget, one needs to be aware of the American practice of opening the American consumer market for drugs to foreign exporters in order to pursue strategic objectives abroad.

The portability of narcotics and the huge price mark up from production to point of sale makes them a particularly useful source of financing for covert operations. Even more important is that the proceeds from narcotics sales fall completely outside conventional, constitutional channels of funding. This helps explain the ubiquitous presence of narcotics trafficking in zones of conflict around the world, from Columbia to Afghanistan.

Little examined, however, is the impact of narcotics trafficking on communities and economies at the point of sale. Consider, for example, the impact on real estate markets and financial services. Real estate is an attractive area in which to employ the cash surplus resulting from narcotics sales because it is, as an industry, entirely unregulated with respect to money laundering. Because cash is an acceptable and in some places familiar method of payment, large sums can be disposed of easily and with little comment. This can and does result in considerable distortion to local demand, and in turn provide fuel for real estate speculation and increased credit demand to finance it along with considerable opportunities for speculation and fraud.

The Iran Contra episode during the 1980s contained all these elements; although many are familiar with the sale of arms to Iran to provide cash to finance CIA backed guerrillas in Nicaragua and death squads in El Salvador, less well-known is the systematic looting of local financial institutions and narcotics sales in the U.S. Banking allows the application of leverage to the cash that is generated by "illegal" activity while simultaneously making it possible to launder the funds. And when a bank fails, it is the shareholders, uninsured depositors and the taxpayer who pick up the bill.

The point here is that narcotics trafficking creates a milieu in which the incentives to engage in uneconomic activity are greater than those to engage in economic activity. In a word, the profits from stealing are higher than the profits from playing by the rules.

What counts from a public policy point of view in the cartelized economy is the ability to control and concentrate cash flows of any kind. To this end, it is less important that a bank fails than that the federal credit is available to make good the losses. In doing so, the cash cost of losses is shifted, or socialized, to the national taxpayer base. As long, therefore, as there are willing lenders to the Federal Government, the game can go on. A short primer on the Federal Reserve seen as **a** criminal enterprise through the eyes of Congressman Louis T. McFadden, at one time the chairman of the House banking Committee may prove enlightening:

> *There is not one man within the sound of my voice who does not know that the Federal Reserve Bank system is the greatest rip-off ever known to man!*

So said a great American patriot, the late Congressman Louis T. McFadden; a courageous statesman-congressman who fought the monstrous cancer upon the American nation for all of his years in Congress. This brave patriot ranks with the great heroes of the United States, a man who paid with his life for daring to expose the flagrant monetary slavery imposed by the Federal Reserve Act of 1913 on the nation he loved.

Two attempts were made to murder McFadden, but they were unsuccessful: the first came when shots were fired at him as he alighted from a cab outside of a Washington hotel. Both missed, the bullets lodging in the bodywork of the cab instead of the intended victim. The second attempt on McFadden's life came via the poison cup. Luckily for McFadden and the American nation, a doctor was present at a dinner he was attending. The doctor was able to secure a stomach pump and snatch McFadden from the jaws of death in the nick of time. The third attempt was also via the poison cup: this time it was successful. Strangely, the death certificate cites the cause of death as "heart failure."

What makes up the corrupt central banking system, and who are the men who run it?

> ➤ Who are these men who hold the American people in slavery?
> ➤ Who are the people who successfully circumvented the United States Constitution?
> ➤ Who are these people who make a mockery of the 4th of July?

In this work I attempt to shed some light on these dark and sinister men and their Whore of Babylon banking system of whom it seems every congressman goes in fear.

When the conspirators of the Federal Reserve were successful in obtaining passage of their monstrous bill and when the 16th Amendment was passed, it closed the chapter on years of plotting to put in place the most terribly efficient method to exploit and rob the American people ever known in the history of mankind.

The concerted efforts by a group of unscrupulous men to overturn the provisions contained in the Constitution of the United States of America, was rewarded by passage of the Federal Reserve Act, which placed power and financial tyranny in the hands of a few, faceless men. It is futile and indeed foolish to talk about liberty and justice as long as the Federal Reserve Bank system is alive and well. We have no liberty, justice or freedom as long as the Federal Reserve remains in place. We are bondsmen in a very real sense, for is it not true that each and every one of us owes the Federal Reserve more that $23,000? That is what they say! Are we burdened down by the so-called "national debt?"

If the answer is "yes" then we are indeed bondsmen, slaves. The Federal Reserve Bank system is built around twelve privately owned banks. A number of banks were hit upon so that it could never be called "a central bank," but nobody was fooled by such Simple Simon trickery.

The private banking monopoly known as the Federal Reserve placed America in the toils of a most hideous taskmaster, far worse than the taskmasters of the Pharaohs of ancient Egypt. The most reprehensible dereliction of duty by the Congress must surely have occurred in 1913, when it gave the power of life and death over the American people to a bunch of men the great writer, H. L. Mencken, described as "low, unmitigated scoundrels."

The Federal Reserve (known as the Fed) banks are modeled on "the Old Lady of Threadneedle Street," (the Bank of England) who's chief architect, J.P. Morgan had always been the fiscal agent for the European monarchy. The banking dynasty built by "old John P" still represents the Fondi, that is to say, the old royal families and their Black Nobility Venetian cousins. This is still very much the way things are in 2007.

The "Fed" was able to rake in enormous profits every year and was not challenged on Constitutional grounds until the advent of McFadden. In 1930 McFadden sued the Federal Reserve for the return of $28 billion, which he said, had been stolen from the American people. The Stark attack by McFadden on the sacred portals of the "Fed" sent Shockwaves coursing up and down Wall Street. It was seen as an unseemly challenge to the Rothschild dynasty, founded by Meyer Amschel Rothschild whose greatest achievement was installing his agent, August Belmont (an assumed name), at the head of the fiscal and monetary affairs of the most powerful nation on Earth. Another Rothschild agent was Alexander Hamilton (also an assumed name) who appeared on the Washington and New York scene from the West Indies.

Hamilton, actually a British intelligence agent, moved swiftly to take command of the monetary policies of the United States with the full cooperation and backing of Belmont. Hamilton and Belmont were able to ingratiate themselves into Wall Street banking circles and the New York social upper-crust society, in an amazingly short space of time. Together, Hamilton and Belmont aided the foundations of what was to become the largest slave state ever known to man, the United States of America. Nobody appeared to mind that "the Fed" was not a reserve bank in the properly understood sense, and that as such, it was a gigantic swindle and a hoax.

This was made possible by a deliberate policy of never teaching even the rudiments of money in our schools and universities, which when combined with threats and intimidation, are enough to keep money "mysterious" and supposedly, hard to understand. A leaderless, spineless Congress only added to the lack of understanding of the basic concepts of "money.'

Congress is still to this day in flagrant dereliction of its duties, because it allows the "Fed" to perpetuate itself at the expense of the American people, knowing full well, that the "Fed" is an illegal institution. How could such a terrifying nightmare have become a reality? How did it all begin? How did the central banks of Europe succeed in subverting the Constitution of the United States—which they hated so much—seemingly right under the nose of Congress, supposedly elected to uphold it? How was it that evil men were able to overcome the one provision of United States law, which was there to protect the American people from the unscrupulous "unmitigated scoundrels" of the central banks of Europe?

Having placed their representatives in key positions in the House and Senate, the European banker, the conspirators, moved ahead rapidly to consolidate the bridgehead they had established.

The only man who saw what they were about was President

Andrew Jackson. Elected on the promise that he would close down the Second United States Bank, the forerunner of today's Federal Reserve Banks, the Second United States Bank was foisted onto Madison and the Republicans in 1816, after years of relentless pressure from Wall Street. Like the First United States Bank, which had a 20-year charter, the Second United States Bank was also privately owned, which held out no benefits for the American people. Its sole purpose was to enrich the bank's stockholders at the expense of the American people, which Jackson was quick to notice.

Jackson was outspoken in his condemnation of the bank, and his strategy of not allowing government money to be deposited in the Second United States Bank was devastatingly successful. His attacks on the bank and its stockholders was swift and without in parallel in the history of banking in the United States. In this Jackson enjoyed the support of the majority of the American people, and when he stood for re-election he was returned to the White House in a blaze of glory. He achieved a great victory for the American people, and promptly vetoed a bill passed by Congress that would have extended the life of the Second United States Bank.

Jackson was tremendously popular with the people. The national debt was wiped out and government actually managed to garner a surplus. Jackson ordered $35 million of the nation's surplus to be distributed among the States, which was the intent of the Framers of the Constitution. What is disturbing is that even in 1832, the bank had congress vote for it. Since then, both the House and Senate have declined to shut down the Federal Reserve and we are regularly treated to the spectacle of our legislators bowing and scraping to the chairman of the "Fed" whomever it happens to be, from Arthur Burns to Alan Greenspan.

It is distressing to witness the way the legislators pull on their collective forelock every time the chairman of the "Fed" is called before committees to testify. I will never forget one particular incident where Volcker sat blowing cigar smoke in the faces of the committee members, while Senator Jake Garn of Utah, liberally bowed before him. But the senators on the committee simply closed their eyes to what Volcker represented, thereby aiding and abetting in the defiling of the Constitution they swore an oath to uphold.

The Constitution is very clear on who should be controlling money:

Article 1 Section 8, Paragraph 5 states:

> "... that only the Congress shall have the power to coin money, regulate the value thereof and of foreign coin."

It goes on to say:

> "No State shall make any thing but gold and silver coin a tender in payment of debts."

Nowhere does the Constitution permit Congress to delegate its authority. The burning issue for every election ought to be the continued existence of the Federal Reserve Board and each and every candidate for whatever office ought to be forced to sign a pledge that he, or she, will vote to abolish the "Fed" if elected, such a pledge to be legally binding. Failure to honor the pledge must be cause for removal of office of the offender.

Those responsible for bringing the Fed to America's shores belong in a rogue's gallery. Salmon P. Chase, J.P. Morgan, Alexander Hamilton, Colonel Mandel House, Aldrich Vreeland, A. Piaff Andew, Paul Warburg, Frank Van Der Lip, Henry P. Davison, Charles D. Norton, Benjamin Strong, President Woodrow Wilson, Arsene Pujo and Samuel Untermeyer, to name a few of the worthy candidates.

These men and their allies on Wall Street did more damage to the young American nation than any foreign army attacking our shores could have ever accomplished. Were we to be invaded and overcome by a foreign power, we could not be more enslaved than we are now, less free, with less reason to believe in the future of the America envisaged by our Founding Fathers. We are caught in the toils of a monstrous swindle of such immense proportions that reasonable men refuse to believe it. The great American patriot William Jennings Bryan cried out against this new form of slavery and condemned the Aristocrats of Paper Money:

> *Congress has the sole power to coin and issue money. We demand that all paper money, which is made legal, be redeemable in coin.*

But like John the Baptist, his was a voice crying in the wilderness. The Federal Reserve Act to was passed by Congress on May 30 1908, following a carefully-crafted and staged "panic" in 1907 of which the chief instigator and architect was Morgan. Even in 2007 Morgan through his chief executive, Dennis Weatherstone still dictates fiscal policy to the Secretary of State on a daily basis, from under the British flag, which flies over Morgan offices in Wall Street.

The 1908 bill was titled the Aldrich Vreeland Emergency Currency Act. The very name was chosen with the intent to deceive the public. There was no emergency. Incidentally, Nelson Aldrich was the grandfather of David Rockefeller, and Edward B. Vreeland was a banker-congressman from New York, who gladly performed the required service for his masters, in violation of his oath to uphold the Constitution. Thus was laid the foundation for war on the people. Let no one reading this message believe otherwise. Establishing the Fed was a declaration of war on the people of the United States.

History reveals three basic types and styles of warfare. The one direct method to make war is through religion, by having the people empty their pockets in obedience to God, who usually turns out to have an earthly address. This method is rather fallible, as disillusionment sets in fairly quickly and it is harder and harder to turn it back. War by means of military conquest is of course, the most easily recognizable method, but costs a great deal of money to sustain occupation of the conquered land, which is never really conquered, unless the implacable hatred for the invaders can be overcome.

In the case of the Bolshevik Revolution, and Mao's China and the Pol Pot of Cambodia, this was accomplished by the murder of millions of people, who were called "counterrevolutionaries and dissidents." The same thing will happen in the United States when our turn comes, as it surely will if we continue to ignore the overbearing domination of the "Fed." Unless we begin to turn our energies away from the television opiates and the drug of mass spectator sport, we are assured a place in history as the largest nation to be subjugated in the history of the world.

The third and perhaps most effective form of warfare is economic warfare. It is correct to say that all wars are economic in origin. Wars are rooted in economics and it has ever been so. In this instance, the conquered population is more pliant and cooperative toward its captors. They enjoy a measure of freedom of movement, of religion, of assembly, and they even go through the farce of electing representatives every two and four years. What we have today in America is not a banking system, but an aberration of one, in which theft on a grand scale is practiced.

The system is thoroughly perverted and run by crooks wearing business suits, ensconced in paneled offices where they hide their identity from the American people. Today, 85 years after the Federal Reserve banking system was thrust through the Congress by the names of the men who control the finances of our country are still not known to us. In these days of "open government" and an abundance of laws forbidding closed doors in public affairs, these carpetbaggers are still able to conduct the banking business of the nation in secret! How is it possible that we, the people, tolerate an ongoing situation where we have no way of knowing who these men are, and thus, we are never able to hold them accountable? The right to coin money and regulate the value thereof belongs exclusively to the people, yet we continue, year after year, to allow the thieves who came in the night, to go on holding the nation to ransom.

The United States operates its monetary and fiscal affairs on worthless, checkbook money and Federal Reserve debt obligations. The real money, the coin of the nation, was always issued by government in days now seemingly gone forever. Now it has passed into the hands of thieves in high places. By means of a ledger entry, the Federal Reserve creates money out of thin air, and then lends it to the U.S. Treasury at usury that is steadily choking the nation to death. Whatever happened to the Bible law that usury is a capital crime? The economic war being waged upon the people of this nation has come to a point where if we do not end it; tremendous changes in our way of life will follow. We are already an enslaved people; all that remains for the Federal Reserve overlords is to make it official.

In 1910, the conspirators felt they were strong to move against the unsuspecting people of the United States. The Sealed Train set off on the evening of November 22, 1910 to lay the groundwork. Like Lenin, they felt that a sealed train was the best way to accomplish total anonymity. The sealed train teamed out of Hoboken, New Jersey, destination Jekyll Island off the coast of Georgia.

Never in history has a more formidable enemy set out to wage war on an unsuspecting nation. Their weapons were treachery, sedition, lies and deceit. Led by Senator Nelson Aldrich, the group consisted of A. Piatt Andrew, Assistant Secretary to the Treasury, Charles D. Norton representing the First National Bank of New York, Frank Van Der Lipp of the National City Bank of New York, Henry P. Davison of J.P. Morgan, Paul Moritz Warburg, Benjamin Strong, and several minor league banking players. So heinous was the scheme upon which they were embarking, so far-reaching was the cause, that I venture to suggest it would exceed the pain and suffering of all the wars in which the U.S. has ever taken part.

The first indication of the group and their Jekyll Island convocation came in an article published by E. C. Forbes in 1916. None of the Jekyll Island participants wrote about their plot. Although Carter-Glass, Warburg and House all wrote volumes about their Frankenstein creation, none of them disclosed the role they played in plot to dispossess the American people of their heritage. There can be no doubt that the leading spirit and the guiding hand was Paul Moritz Warburg, because he had the experience of European central banks lacking in the others.

Aldrich was in my opinion, merely a convenient Warburg messenger boy in the Senate. His only reason for being included in the Jekyll Island Conspiracy was the willingness he had showed to draft the legislation and do the bidding of Warburg and the Wall Street bankers.

Ferdinand Lunberg in his work, *Sixty Families*, stated:

> *The protracted Jekyll Island conference took place in an atmosphere of elaborate secrecy. The trip to Georgia was made in a private car chartered by Aldrich and the travelers all so that the train crew could not establish their identity. For a long time, it was believed that no conclave had been held. The financiers wanted a central bank of the European model to facilitate the large-scale manipulation of the national economy.*

> *An instrument was desired that would function, as had the United States Bank, smashed by Andrew Jackson because it concentrated too much power in private hands. Veteran Nelson Aldrich introduced a scenario produced by the Jekyll Island "duck hunters" that was immediately hooted down as a nefarious Wall Street enterprise and for the time being, came to naught.*

The task of the Wilson administration was essentially to place the measure on the Statute Books, but in an eccentric disguise. The job of drawing up such a bill was given to Warburg, one of the most experienced bankers in the group of plotters. Warburg collaborated with the big financiers on Wall Street, as his memoirs reveal, and when the administration's views were needed, he conferred with Colonel Edward M. House.

The Wall Street draft, superficially revised by Wilson and Carter— Glass was simply the Jekyll Island duck hunter scheme for a central bank dressed in fancy toggery. There was some opposition to it from the uninformed on Wall Street, but it was significantly endorsed by the American banking association. In practice, the Federal Reserve Bank of New York became the fountainhead of a system of twelve regional banks. The other eleven were so many mausoleums created the problem of a central bank and to quell Jacksonian fears in the hinterland and to get around the Constitutional restriction against one central bank.

Could anything be more demeaning than the great United States with its resolve to be free, and which had gone through a major war with England to achieve its objective, now being deceived by a group of treasonous bankers? As I have said elsewhere, and in other publications of mine, American women and children are being forced to go to work in ever-increasing numbers, for less and less pay each year, while their disillusioned, unemployed husbands and fathers are forced to stay at home because there are no jobs for them. Divorce is booming, as is murder of unwanted, unborn children. Abortion has become a legal slaughterhouse, generating a great deal of money for those who run the charnel houses. All this is the work of the Committee of 300 and their servants who are traitors and seditionists, who the Constitution disregards.

The change from the old times when the "crown" alone could issue coin came about by substitution of theology for scientific methods, and philosophy lost its place to corruption and pragmatism, thinly disguised as modem banking methods. We have allowed banks to create something out of nothing. What has man ever created? The answer is, apart from "money," exactly nothing. To create means to make something, previously non-existent. What do we see when it comes to paper money? Our government says it is legal tender. But it is worthless paper on which a series of denominations have been inscribed, so that it can be "tendered" for something of real value, like a home, for instance. But even a home or a house is not created.

It is constructed by man using his ingenuity to change the form of certain substances that were already in existence, substances like clay, silica, timber planking combined with his labor to complete a finished product. It costs something to make a house, but it costs almost nothing for our slave-masters at the "Fed" to "create money." In fact the only cost is the cost of printing it, and even that is mostly borne by someone other than the Federal Reserve. Thus it is not hard to see how is unjust and inequitable is what the Bible calls, "The Whore of Babylon."

Can we do without money? The answer is no, but by the same token, the money maker—the man who by his ingenuity and labor built the house should be—but is not—amply rewarded.

The only way to bring this inequity back to balance is to take the money-creating (as opposed to money-making) power out of the hands of the relatives of the Sealed Train Bandits of Jekyll Island. Unless we can do this, and return the power to create money back to the Congress, we are a doomed nation. When Woodrow Wilson was blackmailed into signing the Federal Reserve Act under the duress of exposure of the Peck love-letters, we, as a nation, lost our birthright and our freedom. That day of infamy when large numbers of our legislators decided it was more important to be home for Christmas than to stand guard against the Barbary Pirate's of Jekyll Island was indeed a day of infamy not rivaled by Pearl Harbor.

"What is so bad, what is so wrong with the Fed?" I am often asked. To start with it, the whole thing is a monstrous lie: It is not a government institution and is illegal because the highest legal authority in the nation, the Constitution, says it is illegal. That makes all of us outlaws, living in an outlaw society. The Federal Reserve steals billions of dollars from the producers of real wealth, by means of imposition of usury (interest) payments, exacting money from the wealth-producers by way of usury (interest) payments.

The bottom line is that we, the people, are obliged to pay a faceless, unknown group of bankers billions of dollars in tribute money.

We pay a group of faceless, swindlers billions in interest on money we are forced to borrow from the very same people to whom we obligingly gave it at no cost in the first instance. Worse yet, in so doing, we hand these bankers the means and the wherewithal to whipsaw our economy in whatever direction the Committee deems desirable.

Chapter 13

The Federal Reserve Coup-d'État

In 1929 the United States was a prosperous country, notwithstanding the disastrous WWI into which Wilson had dragged it. The country had all of the skills and natural resources and ingenuity needed to make it a truly great industrial power in the world. Farmland was plentiful, and fertile, our people willing to work long and hard to produce real wealth in the form of goods and services. But those who participated in the wholesale sell-out of the nation at Jekyll Island were not satisfied. Greed ruled them. By whipsawing the economy hither and thither, the Committee of 300 has succeeded in destroying the American dream by arranging severe shortages of the money supply. The U.S. has have never been enslaved by an invading army, nor have we been stricken by hunger and disease epidemics. Whatever came along, we could handle. But then the money suppliers decided to shut off the money supply at a time when it was most needed to sustain the life-blood of the nation.

What happened in consequence thereof? Our country was decimated. The cultural city of Dresden did not suffer as much from Winston Churchill's murderous firestorm bombing, in the Second World War as America suffered from the 1929–1930's depression.

The Federal Reserve Banks, deliberately and with malice aforethought, shut off $8 billion from the money supply, throwing twenty-five percent of the work force onto the dole. They withheld credit and loans to farmers and businessmen alike. Then when no one could pay, they seized the real wealth of the nation: homes, farms, property and equipment.

In other words, the Federal Reserve Board, the illegal entity, by a real time coup-d'état deprived the nation of its real wealth in goods and services by tightening the money supply, which enabled it to appropriate real property for a song in the post Wall Street crash in the United States. That could happen again at any time. The machinery, which enabled the Federal Reserve to rob us, is still in place, intact today as it was in 1929. Of course, that is what it was designed for.

The Federal Reserve has never been audited. The General Accounting Office (GAO), watchdog of public-money expenditures, has never been allowed to do so. Under pressure from McFadden, The GAO made an effort to audit the Federal Reserve. The audit team was stopped at the doors of the bank by Arthur Burnseig, who went under the assumed name of Arthur Burns. He refused to let the audit team enter the bank. Burns was Secretary of the Treasury at the time; in other words, he was a public servant, but he was acting for his masters, the privately owned Federal Reserve.

I do not want to turn this into a discourse on the technicalities of economics, money, currency and banking, so I will try to confine myself to simple facts. The way the Federal Reserve Banking system is set up allows the bank to gain huge benefits at our expense. That is, in fact, the bottom line of the whole exercise.

Examine the facts and you'll find the cards are stacked against us under the present system. The monetary setup is costly. It charges money (usury) to lend money; that is to say, money used by the community to make real wealth. As such, it is grossly inefficient, benefiting a few and penalizing the majority. It is, in short, designed to create a shortage of money where there is palpably no shortage. This creates social problems, which are being continually compounded, rendering the nation incompatible with good government, social justice, liberty, freedom and a properly constituted social order. In all of this you will find the seeds of revolution. Revolution opens the way for government to suspend provisions of the Constitution. Pretty soon, "1984" will be upon us. For the sake of good order, we will be told that our civil liberties must be suspended. We can easily see how we have been led into a trap from which there is no escape, unless we act before the trap is sprung. What we must realize is that by subtle means, the inalienable right of We, the People, (via our elected representatives) has been subverted. By taking away coin and giving and replacing it with credit and checkbook money, our right to issue that money and the control of the value thereof was transferred to the banking fraternity through their monopoly on credit. The practical effect of the transfer was to place in the hands of unscrupulous men the power to veto the will of the people as expressed through Congress and the President.

If ever there was a near-perfect coup-d'état, this was it.

That is why it is so difficult to apportion blame where it justly belongs. How often have we not heard disgruntled voters vowing never to vote for a President again because his economic policies have failed to work? The truth is a President's economic policies never have the chance to get off the ground.

The president does not control the economic destiny of America. That prerogative belongs to the Federal Reserve. The People, the President, lost the power to control money in 1913, and with it, control of our destiny.

Returning now to the conspirators and their Jekyll Island meeting; Paul Mortiz Warburg was the man who came up with a title for the new central bank. It was Warburg who said that Aldrich was not to use his name in the preamble of the Bill, since this might alert the opposition in Congress, which had previously rejected Aldrich's measures to establish a central bank. Warburg insisted that the provisions of the German Reichsbank be incorporated into the language of the measure; namely, that complete control over interest rates be vested in the Federal Reserve, as well as control over contracting and expanding credit. This was the provision that brought on the 1930's depression. Warburg stated that in his view, the American banking system

"... did violence to almost every banking tenet held sacred in the Old World."

Warburg prevailed, and what Congress so cheerfully signed closely approximated the Constitution of the Reichsbank. Wilson completed the circle of treachery by appointing Warburg to be the first Federal Reserve chairman, a post which he continued to hold even after Wilson dragged America into war with Germany, Warburg's native land. Such is the power of the One World, One Government conspiracy. No sacrifice of others is too great for them, no goal unattainable, no one safe from their machinations, whether he be the President of the United States or a lesser light. Now one would think that government and our Congressional representatives would be eager, if not downright anxious, to bring the truth about the Federal Reserve to the attention of the public. Nothing could be further from the truth. The crime of secretly altering the money laws of the United States was concealed from the people. In my view there can be no greater crime than that. Pliny the historian calls such actions "a crime against mankind." By concealing the true intent and purpose of the Federal Reserve Act of 1913 from the people, Congress and the American Banking Association were guilty of a heinous crime against humanity.

Alexander Hamilton voted to adopt European Central Banking system methods and inserting them into banking laws in the United States, thereby considerably helping to subvert the US Constitution, which forbad a central bank. Hamilton wittingly subverted the will of the framers of the Constitution to be circumvented at the behest of his master, Rothschild. Hamilton aided and abetted in altering conditions, which subsequently provided a fertile climate for the giving birth of the greatest banking monopoly known to man, to wit, the Federal Reserve.

With our monetary system locked into a permanently unsound and unstable condition from which it cannot escape, there is little hope of ever becoming a truly free people. Early 1800s, trade cycles were absolutely unknown, because they simply could not occur under monetary policies, which were followed right up to the end of that century. What "our" system does now is guarantee deflation by trying to hold it back through credit policies that raise prices and actually increase the chances of inflation. Interest (usury) is the other cause of trade cycles, our Western economics being founded on debt, a situation which can, and will, lead to the destruction of civilization. Today in America, we are preoccupied with social justice, but we cannot have social justice until the Federal Reserve is closed down and the national debt abolished by an act of Congress. How can any nation survive, let alone make progress, when the following monetary situations prevail? What follows is an open conspiracy which legislators know about, but will do nothing to end.

> ➤ The issue of money and the control of its value are in the hands of a private monopoly, run by men who are not known to the people.
> ➤ The highest executive in the country, the President, has no control over the Federal Reserve, no input, and no authority to intervene in any of its affairs, save to appoint the chairman.
> ➤ Any economic policies the President makes can be thwarted or sabotaged by the Federal Reserve private bank controllers.
> ➤ That same bank receives almost gratis all the money it needs from our government. Yet, when our government needs the money for the people, it has to borrow that money from the Federal Reserve Bank at interest (usury), which it has to pay back in the form of interest-bearing bonds. These bonds are never retired, even when fully paid off. This is a gigantic fraud.
> ➤ As a result of fraudulent transaction, the people are forced deeper and deeper into debt, while the President is powerless to do anything about it and the people's

representatives are unwilling to put an end to it.
- ➤ The banker's monopoly is allowed to create money at will. They create money out of nothing by simply making ledger entries.
- ➤ No audit is ever made of the Federal Reserve.

John Adams, one of the founders of the Republic, once stated:

All the perplexity, confusion and distress in America not from the defects of the Constitution of Confederation, not from want or honor or virtue, so much as from downright ignorance of the nature of coin, credit and circulation.

That is certainly one of the most accurate statements ever made. In the *Book of Solomon*, we read the following:

The borrower is servant of the lender.

We as a nation, a proud people, are now quite simply the servants of the lender, the Federal Reserve. As servants, we have no status. That is why it is pointless to celebrate the 4th of July.

Jesus Christ said:

Verily, verily, I say unto you, the servant is not greater than his Lord.

- ➤ So what do we celebrate on the 4th of July?
- ➤ Our status as servants?
- ➤ Or is it our freedom, which we lost in 1913?
- ➤ Our continuing financial enslavement?

Here now are a few quotations to think about. The first one is from President Woodrow Wilson, who in his latter life bitterly regretted ever signing the Federal Reserve Act into power and lamented that fact on his deathbed:

A great industrial nation is controlled by its system of credit. Our system of credit is concentrated. The growth of the nation and all our activities are in the hands of a few men. We have come to be one of the worst ruled, one of the most completely controlled and dominated governments in the world; no longer a government of free opinion, no longer a government by conviction and vote of the majority, but a government by the opinion and the duress of small groups of dominant men.

And Wilson said just before he died, "I *have betrayed my country.*"

Sir Josiah Stamp, who was President of the Bank of England in the 1920's and who was the second richest man in England:

Banking was conceived in iniquity and was born in sin. The Bankers on earth; take it away from them but leave them in power to create deposits, and with the flick of the pen they will create enough deposits to gain it back again. However, take it away from them and all the great fortunes, like mine, will disappear, and they ought to disappear from this world, for it would be a happier and a better place to live in. But if you wish to remain the slaves of the bankers and pay the cost of your own slavery, let them continue to create deposits.

Robert H. Hemphill, a one-time credit manager of the Federal Reserve banking system in Atlanta, Georgia (this was, of course, after he left office):

This is a staggering thought: we are completely dependent on the commercial banks. Someone has to borrow every dollar we have in circulation, cash or credit. If the banks create ample synthetic money, we prosper. If not, we starve. We are absolutely without a permanent money system. When one gets a complete grasp of the picture, the tragic absurdity of our hopeless position is almost incredible, but there it is. It is so important that our present civilization may collapse unless it becomes widely understood and the defects remedied very soon.

Congressman Louis T. McFadden:

> *The Federal Reserve Banks are now one of the corrupt institutions the world has ever seen.*

The Federal Reserve comes under one general heading, and I'll give you a brief summary of how it is constituted. I will quote from their own publication:

> *The Federal Reserve System comprises the Board of Governors, the Federal Open Market Committee, the Federal Advisory Council, and the member banks. The system's function lies in the field of money, credit and banking. The Federal Reserve System was organized in 1914.*
>
> *Responsibility for the Federal Reserve policy and decisions rests on the Board of Governors, the Federal Open Market Committee and the Federal Advisory Council.*

(Please note that the responsibility does not rest with the President or the Congress. It rests with these bank officials).

> *In some matters, the law puts primary responsibility on the Board, in some on the reserve banks, and in some on the Committee, though in practice there is close coordination of action.*
>
> *Accordingly for the sake of simplicity, the term "Federal Reserve Authorities" is frequently used when it is unnecessary to indicate, which of the three is responsible for action or to what extent the responsibility is shared. The Federal Open Market Committee comprises the seven members of the Board of Governors and five representatives of the Federal Reserve Banks.*
>
> *The Committee directs the open market operations of the Federal Reserve Banks; that is, the purchases and sales of United States government securities and other obligations in the open market. The purpose of these operations is to maintain a basis for bank credit ample to meet the business*

needs of the country.

The Federal Advisory Council consists of 12 members, one selected annually by each Federal Reserve Bank through its board of directors. The Council meets in Washington at least four times a year.

It confers with the Board of Governors on general business conditions and makes recommendations regarding the affairs of the Federal Reserve System. Its recommendations are purely advisory.

Please note, that our elected representatives in the House and Senate have no say or no control over what these faceless men do with our economy.

It is the Open Market Committee, which, more than any other division runs this country. It is but a carefully crafted front behind which hides one man who runs the open market account and is therefore in a position to know the rise and fall of the stock market because he plans it.

As Congressman Wright Patman once said:

The Open Market Committee chairman knows every dip and rise in the stock market before it happens, and he can give others tips which will enable them to make millions overnight; and does, of course, to his friends.

We should bring this thing to an end: of a few people to make interest high and bonds low, to manipulate the monetary system of our nation in a way that speculators are enriched and fare better than honest people who work for a living. That then, is the true function of the Open Market Committee, laid bare for all to see. I'd like to quote you, too, from Mr. Thomas A. Edison, as follows:

People who will not turn a shovel full of dirt on the project (talking about the Muscle Shoals dam), nor contribute a pound of material will collect more money from the United States than will the people who supply all the material and do all the work. This is the terrible thing about interest.

But here is the point: if the nation can issue a dollar bond, it can also issue a dollar bill. The element that makes the bond good makes the bill good also.

The difference between the bond and the bill is that the bond lets the money broker collect twice the amount of the bond and additional 20 percent, whereas the currency, the honest sort provided by Constitution.

It is absurd to say our country can issue bonds and cannot issue currency. Both are promises to pay, but one fattens the usurer and the other helps the people. If the currency issued by the people were no good, then the bonds would be no good either. It is a terrible situation when the government, to insure the national wealth, must go into debt and submit to ruinous interest charges at the hands of men who control the fictitious value of gold. Interest is the invention of Satan.

Of course we all know that the Bible and the Koran and other books are absolutely opposed to interest, but we got away from all those things and that's how we got into the mess we are in today. What we are left with now is a shell of a country, which but for the Federal Reserve swindle, would be the most powerful in the world, beyond belief, with liberty and justice for all. We are slaves unless we are prepared to henceforth to make it our business, night and day, to force Congress to put an end to the Federal Reserve Banking System and end our enslavement. Who actually owns the Federal Reserve Banks? Since it is incorporated, it should be a relatively easy matter to obtain a list of the stockholders, but as far as I am aware no one has yet succeeded in getting this information.

How is this continuing fraud perpetrated? Government's power combined with advancing computer technology has vastly simplified the task of managing the national—and by extension the international—cash flow. Politically, the American victory in the Second World War meant that the entire West and its dependencies were co-opted into the International Monetary

Fund (IMF) negotiated at the Bretton Woods Conference in 1944. Forty-five years later, the collapse of the Soviet Union in 1989 meant that for the first time in history there was no alternative monetary or political choice in the international arena. The British Empire had surrendered to the Americans precisely because America represented an alternative to sterling, namely the dollar.

The U.S. presides over a more or less fully closed global monetary system centered on the dollar. In practice this means that those countries within the system must exchange real value in the form of manufactured goods and commodities with the U.S. cartel in exchange for currency that is not a real dollar, but a Federal Reserve note incorrectly called a dollar, which is no more than an accounting entry created "money" out of thin air. This is analogous to a company with no assets exchanging worthless stock for cash and indeed this is no accident. It was a favored technique by which the J.P. Morgan family of the nineteenth century successfully financed the consolidation of American industry and finance. Today their heirs are busily dong the same thing, but on a global scale.

The rapid technological advance has ruled out the possibilities for creative management in banking. Its sheer number-crunching power has rendered the cost of iterative calculations to more or less zero. This has enabled the creation of a new sector in the industry, the derivatives business, which is nothing more than the breaking down of financial instruments such as stocks and bonds into their constitutive parts, and tripled the power of the banks, courtesy of the fully-fledged cooperation of the Federal Reserve and Congress, who have allowed the banks to not only self-regulate their derivatives portfolios and businesses but have enacted rules to force other banks to use derivatives to "control" risk. In practice this has meant that the most profitable business of the banks has been moved off balance sheet, in effect creating a high level of secrecy in their business. It also confers a huge advantage on the largest banks to who the others have to come for their derivatives. This has, in part, fuelled the manic consolidation in banking and has been applied with tremendous success internationally thanks to the imposition of the Basel Accords on money and banking, which have forced other country's financial institutions to either cooperate, which in practice has largely meant be acquired, or go out of business.

The banks' tactics have been copied and refined by industry. An excellent example of this is the case of Enron, nominally an industrial company engaged in the production and transport of petroleum and natural gas, but which was transformed into a highly leveraged financial operation with a huge off balance sheet business trading derivatives. It secured a release from regulatory oversight by the time-tested method of purchasing lawmakers and by suborning its auditors. This gave it the power to restate earnings, virtually at will, simply by changing the assumptions on future interest rates embedded in the options, swaps and futures contracts constituting its unregulated derivatives book.

Enron is a model also of the increasingly blurred distinction between the public and private sector. It employed as many as twenty CIA officers.

One of its senior executives, Thomas White, was an army general before joining Enron and then left Enron to become Secretary of the Army. Enron executives were intimately involved with Vice President Richard Cheney's energy task force. It is difficult to avoid concluding that Enron was anything other than a money-laundering operation employed in the interest of "National Security" on behalf of the cartel. The U.S. has embarked on a costly global military adventure the outcome of which is anything but certain.

This marks the culmination of more than fifty years of nearly continuous overt and covert warfare. In this it is supported by the most sophisticated financing apparatus in history, capable of mobilizing the cash generated from a wide variety of activities both open and covert. The price has been the progressive hollowing out of the American economy itself, and the progressive erosion of civil liberties and the rule of law. The black budget is not the cause of this but the means.

Chapter 14

The Conspiracy of Free Trade

The U.S. formerly a superpower until afflicted with "new world economy" syndrome has lost so much manufacturing capability that it can scarcely build one submarine every two years and one aircraft carrier every five years. How then can we call ourselves "the World's only Superpower"? The American Shipbuilding journal said in 1998 that more manufacturing of ship components and systems will migrate to China in the next five years and it has proved to be very accurate.

"No cause for concern," say the free trade economist's experts. "Shipbuilding is just one of those old manufacturing things that the nanotech U.S. economy is better off without." Sadly according to Manufacturing & Technology News (July 8, 2006) so much manufacturing capability has already left that American nanotechnology capability is largely limited to pilot-scale, low—volume manufacturing and even that is disappearing at an alarming rate.

The day is not far off when we will have to ask China or Russia to build our implements of war for us. In testimony before the House Science Subcommittee on Research, Matthew Nordan of Lux Research, Inc. said that any American nanotech ideas are likely to "be implemented in manufacturing plants on other shores." Nordan said that in some fields of nanotech materials "the manufacturing train has already left the station."

The U.S. may even be falling behind in generating nanotech

ideas. In 2006, China led the world in nanotech research, producing 14%. Even South Korea and Taiwan spend more per capita on nanotech R&D than the U.S. Once the world's leading machine tool manufacture; the U.S. now sits in 17th place behind little Switzerland. Sean Murdock, executive director of the Nano Business Alliance, testifying before a Congressional subcommittee that the U.S. could not live on ideas alone.

Murdock said:

> Intellectual property is fine ... but if you look at the total value associated with any product, most of the value tends to accrue to those that are closest to the customer—those that in fact, make it.

Common sense went out of the window when Wilson was brought into the White House. The first thing Wilson did was to call for a joint session of the House and Senate during which time he berated and harangued the tariff protection that had secures a unique middle class market.

Important as an intellectual property is to the manufacturing process, it is the ability to manufacture and turn a new principle into tangible goods that can be traded. Without the ability to translate an idea into a manufactured product based on the new idea, the possibility of reaping most of the economic rewards would be lost, and with that stultifying condition, the ability to think new ideas (creative abilities) would eventually dry up. Without manufacturing abilities and knowledge, it is difficult to recognize promising nanotech innovations. Put in another way, if you gave a Pre-Historic man a blue print on how to manufacture a rifle to hunt with, it would not change his condition.

For two decades I have stressed over and over again the erosion of the United States middle class, conditions on which free trade has fed since Adam Smith tried to sell British goods to the

Colonists in a one-way deal. Production functions based on acquired knowledge, which has gone to what used to be called "under-developed countries" like China for instance. What is known as the lack of uniqueness required for the operation of comparative advantage, and the international mobility of capital and technology allows those factors of production to seek absolute advantage abroad in skilled, disciplined, low-cost labor. In fact as I have said repeatedly, free trade is a lie and was always a lie from the day that Adam Smith of the East India Company tried to force it on the new American colonies. Free trade has destroyed the unique middle class that made America a great nation; the middle class is a fast vanishing breed.

Thus, once the U.S. trade barriers were removed and the high speed Internet was up and running, first world living standards were no longer protected by unique accumulations of capital and technology. The changed conditions made it possible for American companies to use employees drawn from large excess supplies of foreign labor such exist in India and China today, as cheaper substitutes for better-paid American employees. The difference in labor cost is all-pervasive. Anyone who says the difference is irrelevant does not have the facts. Can an American family live on $200 a month like so many Far Eastern and Indian families are doing?

Nevertheless, as I emphasized in 1972 more than three decades before, India, China and the Philippines became an alternative for U.S. companies; the U.S. is severely disadvantaged for tax reasons as well. Because of tax reasons the U.S. has a high cost of capital.

The American Producers Council Coalition recently stated the problem to the President's Advisory Panel on Federal Tax Reform. Every major trading partner of the U.S., including every other OECD country and China, relies on border-adjusted taxes that abate taxes on their exports to the U.S., while taxing U.S. goods imported from the U.S.

This discrimination is reinforced by the U.S. tax system, which imposes no appreciable tax burden on foreign goods and services sold in the U.S., but imposes a heavy tax burden on U.S. producers of goods and services regardless of whether they are sold within the U.S. or exported to other countries.

The solution is to abandon the income tax and replace it with a value-added or sales tax or even tariffs, or an export-deductible tax. But the New World Order proponents inside the U.S. government are doing everything to bring the level of U.S. living standards down to a much lower level, so this is not likely to be allowed.

The Founding Fathers based U.S. income on tariffs. Tariffs also helped the U.S. develop its industry by protecting its products from competition from lower cost producers abroad. George Washington said tariffs had to be kept in place to protect "American manufactories." But then, along came International Socialist President Wilson, and very his first act was to call for a joint session of the House and Senate and make known his goal of destroying the tariff system that had performed so brilliantly up until his catastrophic ascendancy to the White House.

The intolerably bitter fruits of the Wilson presidency are still being tasted to this very day. An example of this was the March-April pet-food scare that led to a serious crisis when it spread to humans. The *Chicago Tribune* of April 29, 2007 covered the crisis in lengthy report:

> *California officials have revealed that the contamination got into the food chain. About 45 state residents ate pork from hogs that consumed animal feed laced with melamine from China. Melamine is used to make plastics, but it also artificially boosts the protein level-and thus the price of glutens that go into food. It was already fatal for some pets ... 57 brands of cat food and 83 brands of dog food have been recalled. On top of that 6,000 hogs had to be destroyed because they ate tainted food. The effects of melamine on*

people are thought to be minimal, but no one really knows. Its consumption by humans is so improbable that no one has even studied it.

... The importer of the bad wheat gluten Chem-Nutra Inc of Las Vegas, contends that its Chinese manufacturer, illicitly added melamine to the gluten to boost the measurable protein level and thus the price of the shipment.

Those who felt that the Food and Drug Administration (FDA) would catch any such developments were of course, sadly wrong. But in a statement, the FDA said that "food safety funding" for the Agency's Center for Food Safety from $48 million in 2003 to about $30 million in 2006.

Full time jobs at the Center had been cut from 950 in 2003 to 820 in 2006. Even as the tainted wheat gluten cases have multiplied, the FDA has learned of another problem: Chinese rice protein. And now there is another scare emanating from Chinese manufactured toys exported to the U.S. First reports indicate that the toys were painted with lead paint, which has led to a massive recall.

The Founding Fathers' system of custom tariffs was overturned by Wilson and his Socialist advisors, especially the Fabian Society members (forefathers of today's Neo-Bolsheviks also known by the oxymoron "neoconservative" label, who falsely stated that tariffs fell heavily on the poor while benefiting rich manufacturers.

An income tax was seen as a fairer distribution of the tax burden and as the way towards more equality in the distribution of income. Wilson and his controllers did not tell the Congress that this was a Marxist doctrine a long political-ideological struggle ensued that overthrew the tariff system and delivered the unique American middle class into serfdom.

Today income distribution is more unequal than ever. If you, dear reader, think you are not a serf, see what happens if you claim the products of your labor as your own and refuse to pay property taxes. Make sure that you have a good moving company contracted and an alternative place to stay and a parachute before you jump off that cliff. What is needed is an immediate return to the tariff system to raise revenues and the sooner the better. Are there any "Brave-hearts" among the sovereign people?

What we saw with the installation of the Federal Reserve Bank was the consolidation of the grip of the Committee of 300 on America. It followed the American foreign policy and the wars that America has fought over the course of the twentieth century (including the Spanish American War in 1898 and the present so— called War on Terror) have successfully extended the cartel's control over the world economy. Without the successful establishment of a Central Bank in the United States, the wars that were waged after 1912 would never have been possible to wage.

Franklin D. Roosevelt told his political associates that he wanted his legacy to be the champion of the poor who ended the Great Depression. Roosevelt took credit for establishing the social security system, which he passed off as a gain for the people. But he failed to tell the majority of Americans how it was to be funded; through a highly regressive tax on its beneficiaries.

The establishment of the ESF was an extension of the same logic behind the creation of the Federal Reserve in 1914. The latter, the Federal Reserve was also created in response to a crisis: the crash of 1907. The Wall Street legend credits J.P. Morgan's genius and patriotism with saving the Nation. In reality, the crash and resulting depression enabled Morgan to destroy his competitors, buy up their assets and in the process revealed to the nation and the world just how powerful the banks and Morgan were. Not all were grateful, and some demanded legislative action to bring the federal credit and national monetary system under public oversight and control.

In a campaign of masterful political quackery, the Federal Reserve was created in 1912 by an act of Congress to do just this. But by creating it as a private corporation owned by the banks; Congress effectively ceded to the banks a position even stronger than they had occupied before.

Even today it is not widely understood that the Federal Reserve is a privately held business owned by the very interests that it nominally regulates. Thus the control of federal credit and the U.S. monetary system and the rich flow of insider information that results from that control are veiled from public view and are privately controlled in secret, which rather explains the Delphic nature of the Federal chairman.

The Narcotics Trade: Physical Slavery

It may seem strange to think of a positive connection between narcotics trafficking and the stock market, but consider that; in the late 90's the U.S. Department of Justice estimated that the proceeds of such trade entering the U.S. banking system were between $500 and $1,000 billion annually, or more than 5–10% of GDP.

Now the proceeds of crime need to find a way into legitimate, that is legal, channels or they are worthless to the holders. Little examined, however, is the impact of narcotics trafficking on communities and economies at the point of sale. Consider for example, the impact on real estate markets and financial services. Real estate is an attractive area in which to employ the cash surplus resulting from narcotics sales because it is, as an industry, entirely unregulated with respect to money laundering. Because cash is an acceptable and in some places familiar method of payment, large sums can be disposed of easily and with little comment. This can and does result in considerable distortion to local demand, and in turn provide fuel for real estate speculation and increased credit demand to finance it along with considerable opportunities for speculation and fraud.

The government's power combined with advancing computer technology has over the last thirty years made simple the managing of national—and by extension the international—cash flow.

Politically, the American victory in the Second World War meant that the entire West and its dependencies were co-opted into the International Monetary Fund (IMF) negotiated at Bretton Woods in 1944. Forty-five years later, the collapse of the Soviet Union in 1989 meant that for the first time in history there was no alternative monetary or political choice in the international arena. The British Empire had surrendered to the Americans precisely because America represented an alternative to sterling, namely the dollar.

Today the U.S. presides over a more or less fully closed global monetary system based on the dollar. In practice this means that those countries within the system must exchange real value in the form of natural resources like oil and gas, manufactured items and commodities with the U.S. cartel in exchange for dollars, which are no more than an accounting entry created out of thin air. This is analogous to a company with no assets exchanging watered stock for cash, and indeed this is no accident. It was a favored technique by which the J.P. Morgan dynasty of the nineteenth century successfully financed the consolidation of American industry and finance.

Today their heirs are busily doing the same thing, but on a global scale. And it is all out in the open, beyond the conspiracy stage. Because of its unique finance control, the U.S. has been able to embark on costly global military adventures the outcome of which is far from certain.

This marks the culmination of more than fifty years of continuous overt and covert warfare. In this it is supported by the most sophisticated financing apparatus in history, capable of mobilizing the cash generated from a wide variety of activities both open and covert. The price has been the progressive hollowing out of the American economy itself, and the progressive erosion of civil liberties and the rule of law. It will also be the end of this Republic.

Chapter 15

A Means to an End

Who are the planners and plotters who serve the mighty, all powerful Committee of 300? The better-informed of our citizens are aware that there is a conspiracy and that the conspiracy goes under various names. What is not generally recognized is that the well-organized Committee of 300 has now progressed to what MI6 operative H.G. Wells called this phase "The Open Conspiracy." One might say that the conspiracy has served its purpose. The world is now in the next stage, what I call *"beyond the conspiracy."*

The next stage can be put into operation because the American people are in a state of profound shell-shock and are so fully controlled by long range penetration and inner-directional conditioning that they now accept things they would not have accepted even a short ten years ago. Therefore, the conspirators feel they can come out into the open. They no longer need to hide. The populace has been so brainwashed and so conditioned that the whole plot is hardly ever thought of as a "conspiracy."

Today in 2007, it is very much of an open conspiracy with no less a personage than the President of the United States openly proclaiming the dawning of the New World Order, which coming he eagerly, awaits.

That New World Order is a work-in-progress; a revised form of International Communism, a brutal and savage dictatorship that will plunge the world into the New Dark Ages. The Davignon Plan I first announced to the U.S. in 1982 is now in full flower; the United States is about half-way to a conversion to a modern version of a feudal society.

Our steel industry is dead; and our machine-tool industry is dead. Our manufacturing entities shoe-manufacturers, clothing, light industrial equipment, electronics industries, have been exported to foreign countries. The American family farm is lost to "300" food controllers like Archer Daniels Midland, Nestle, and the Bunge Corporation. The American people can now easily be starved into submission should the need ever arise. The leader in this drive to establish a totalitarian state, a New World Order inside a One World Government is quickly emerging as the United States of America, which role it first assumed when the Committee of 300 appointed Woodrow Wilson to the White House.

In November 2005 the United States suffered the most massive trade imbalance in its history. As much as 85 percent of the items formerly manufactured in the United States are now made in foreign countries and imported into the United States. The latest statistics show that Ford Motors will cut 30,000 jobs and General Motors the same number of jobs. These jobs are lost. They are not temporary lay-offs but jobs that will vanish, never to return. The American people have been so conditioned that most cannot see that what is happening to manufacturing jobs being lost in record numbers relates directly to the myth of "free trade" first pressed by the British East India Company in the 18th century.

I quote the profound statement made by the prophet Hosea, which is found in the Christian Bible: "My *people perish for lack of knowledge.*" (The word is actually "information").

So many already have read my expose of the foreign aid scandal, in which work I named several conspiratorial organizations, whose numbers are legion that I feel the subject can be excluded from this book.

Their final objective is the overthrow of the U.S. Constitution and the merging of this country, chosen by God as HIS country, with a godless New World Order—One World Government, which will return the world to feudal conditions far worse than those which existed in the Dark Ages.

Let us talk about actual case histories, the attempt to communize and de-industrialize Italy. The Committee of 300 long ago decreed that there shall be a smaller—much smaller—and better world, that is, their idea of what constitutes a better world. The myriads of what Bertrand Russell called "useless eaters" consuming scarce natural resources are being culled. Industrial progress supports population growth. Therefore, the command to multiply and subdue the Earth found in Genesis has to be subverted through destruction of the industrial employment market, the only stable source of long-term jobs. This calls for a frontal attack upon Christianity; the slow but sure disintegration of industrial nations states; the destruction of hundreds of millions of people, referred to by the Committee of 300 as "surplus population," and the removal of any leader who dares to stand in the way of the Committee's global planning to reach the foregoing objectives.

Three of the Committee's earliest targets were Argentina, Italy and Pakistan. Many other nation states were to be obliterated most notably South Africa, Palestine, Serbia and Iraq. Nations states are to be discouraged and their break-up accelerated, especially if they have aspirations of becoming industrialized.

In order to get an idea of how vast and how all-pervasive is the New World Order conspiracy, it would be appropriate at this point to state the goals set by the Committee of 300 for the pending conquest and control of the world. Once this is understood one can see how one central conspiratorial body is able to operate successfully and why it is that no power on earth can withstand their driving onslaught against the very foundations of a civilized world, based on freedom of the individual, especially as it is declared in the United States Constitution.

How did the Committee of 300 come into existence?

> What is the source of its immense wealth and power?
> How does the Committee maintain its grip upon the world, and more especially, their choke-hold on the United States and Britain?
> One of the most asked questions is "How can any single entity know at all times what is going on and how is control exercised?"

The following statement made by Aurellio Peccei, a senior executive of the Committee of 300, helps to understand where the "300" are coming from:

> *For the first time since the first millennium was approached in Christendom, large masses of people are really in suspense about the impending advent of something unknown which could change their collective fate entirely... Man does not know how to be a truly modern man. Man invented the story of the Bad Dragon, but if ever there was a bad dragon, it is man himself... Here we have the human paradox man trapped by his extraordinary capacity and achievements, as in a quicksand. The more he uses his power, the more he needs it.*

> *We must never tire of repeating how foolish it is to equate the present profound pathological state and maladjustment of the entire human system to any cyclic crisis or passing circumstances.*

> *Since man has opened Pandora's Box of new technologies, he has suffered uncontrolled human proliferation, the mania for growth, energy crises, actual or potential resource scarcities and degradation of environment, nuclear folly and a host of related afflictions.*

The expression "New World Order" is perceived by newcomers as something that developed as a consequence of the Gulf War in 1991, whereas the idea of a One World Government is recognized as being centuries old. In fact it had its origin with the

East India Company (EIC) chartered by Queen Elizabeth I in 1600 as a joint stock company. In 1661 Charles II (Stuart king) gave royal assent to the company that granted among other rights, the right to wage war and make peace with nations.

That enabled the EIC to gain full control of India including lucrative opium trade carried on in Benares and the Ganges Valley by the princes of India. By 1830 all of India was under control of what had become the British East India Company (BEIC). Therein are found the seeds of the beginning of the New World Order.

The New World Order is not new; it has been around developing under one or another guise for a very long time. Its "father" was the London Mercer Company and its grandfather the London Staplers extending back to the German Hansa and the Hansa of Belgium, all the way back to India. From this background came the East India Company, some of whose board members were from the Anabaptist communists, many of who immigrated to England.

During the Colonial period, a number of prominent Anabaptists emigrated from England to the United States. All these factions and diverse cults embraced a common goal, the establishment of an authoritarian New World Order. But it is still even today in 2007, perceived as a development of the future, which is not the case; the New World Order is past and present. All future planning by the Committee's institutions were predicated upon getting rid of 2.5 billion "useless eaters" to paraphrase Lord Bertrand Russell, a senior spokesman of the "300." Natural resources would have to be allocated under the auspices of global planning. Nation states could either accept Club of Rome domination, or else survive by the law of the jungle.

What are the goals of the secret elite conspirators? This elite group also calls itself the *Olympians* because they truly believe they are equal in power and stature to the legendary gods of

Olympus. Like Lucifer their god, they have set themselves above the true God believing they have been charged with implementing the following by divine right:

> Establish a One World Government-New World Order with a unified church and monetary system under their direction all national identities and national boundaries of nations and bring about the destruction of the Christian religion.

> Establish the ability to control of each and every person through means of mind control and bring an end to all industrialization and the production of nuclear generated electric power in what they call "the post-industrial zero— growth society."

> Exempted were the computer-and service industries. United States industries that remain would be exported to countries such as Mexico and the Far East where abundant slave labor is available. As we saw in 1993, this has become a fact through the passage of the North American Free Trade Agreement, known as NAFTA. Free trade was to be the norm of the future

> Suppress all scientific development except for those deemed beneficial by the Committee. Especially targeted is nuclear energy for peaceful purposes.

> Collapse of the world's economies and engender total political chaos. Take control of all foreign and domestic policies of the United States and give the fullest support to supranational institutions such as the United Nations; the International Monetary Fund; the Bank of International Settlements and the World Court to supplant and undermine the U.S. Constitution before abolishing it altogether.

> To penetrate and subvert all governments, and work from within them to destroy the sovereign integrity of the nations represented by them, under the guise of spreading "democracy" as a bulwark against terrorism.

> To organize a world-wide terrorist apparatus and to negotiate with lawful government for their surrender

wherever terrorist activities take place, by allowing the U.S. to establish permanent military bases in those nations.

➢ To take control of education in America with the intent and purpose of utterly and completely destroying it through "graduated change" in curricula and teaching methods. By 1993, the full force and effect of this policy was becoming apparent, and will be even more destructive as primary and secondary schools begin to teach "Outcome Based Education" (OBE).

At best, from his school days, the American man is aware that the United States has a 250-year history, but only in the most tenuous sense and lacking in detail. His knowledge of the Constitution is minimal. He is totally oblivious of the fact that seemingly unrelated incidents and "accidents" of history are in fact closely related and that they were engineered and brought about by a hidden force; the French Revolution instigated by two Masonic Lodges; the rise of Napoleon and the Napoleonic Wars, controlled by the Rothschilds; the "accident" of the brutal, savage First World War, the Bolshevik Revolution and the rise of Communism carefully planned. This bears no relation to the history he was taught at school, which has it that these were unrelated events with no direct connection. He was taught that the great events in the history of the world, including the United States came from nowhere and suddenly sprang into being as if by magic. There has not been a single occasion when he was taught that these shattering events were created and channeled with great precision and manipulated to bisect with pre-set goals. The great conspiracy has never been revealed to him, and if by chance it is mentioned, it is derided as the thinking of crackpots.

Controlled education does not allow for such studies. It is taboo. The nature of the law of contracts is not known to him. Especially political contracts known as "treaties" which, he is told "are the law of the land." Few lawyers understand this is not the case and so we Americans believe that events just occur in a vacuum.

Were he to have the privilege of entering the great repository of knowledge, that is the British Museum, and to spend two years reading with intent to study the back issues of the great newspapers of Britain and the United States, the *New York Times*, the *London Times*, the *Telegraph* starting in late 1890; *Punch* and *The New Yorker* magazines of the 1900s, he would be appalled to find himself looking at the almost identical political format as the *New York Times*, the *Washington Post* and the *London Times* of 2005.

Even more shocking would be his discovery that he was reading the same cliches that he had just read in the old back issues and that they were remarkably similar in design and context in that they preached the message of Communism, the New World Order and a One World Government.

The language would be a little different, the personalities changed over the years, but the tenor and the thrust of the propaganda was the same. If he closed his eyes and reflected on the 1910 paper he was holding in his hands, he would see that it resembled, remarkably and unmistakably, 2007's news. He would be forced to come to the inescapable conclusion that the intent and purpose was to establish first Socialism and then Communism as the systems of a New World Order. For there to be such undoubted consistency, there has to be a high degree of certainty that some high-ranking personages and their entities, must be controlling world events and the events in his own country, the United States of America. Delving further into the colonial history of Great Britain, he might even come across the name of the British East India Company as a power group of the elite who were able to arrange an astonishing array of events.

To establish Socialism in the United States with the purpose of nullifying State Constitutions and the Federal Constitution.

One of the astonishing events managed by the British East India

Company was the establishment of Socialism as a political system. One of the products of the East India Company was the Fabian (Socialist) Society of London. Its leaders, Beatrice and Sydney Webb, Annie Besant, G. D. H. Cole, Ramsey McDonald, Bertrand Russell and H. G. Wells, Thomas Davidson and Henry George whose mother was of the American Liberal Establishment Pratt family of Philadelphia, owed their positions to "the Company." The Pratt Family was closely tied to the East India Company's "trade" with India and held significant interests in the Rockefeller Standard Oil Empire.

Beatrice and Sydney Webb went on to found the London School of Economics in 1895, through which passed some of the most important figures in British and American politics, business, and government. The distinguished alumnus included David Rockefeller, erstwhile president of the National Republican Club, Chairman of the Rockefeller Standard Oil Company, and the leading financier of the infamous Institute for Pacific Relations (IPR), a British East India Company—Committee of 300 spinoffs that provided funding for the Japanese attack on Pearl Harbor on December 7, 1941. He was also the mentor of George Herbert Walker Bush and John F. Kennedy.

Of interest is Beatrice Webb, the dominant partner in the enterprise. One of three daughters of Richard Potter, a wealthy railroad magnate who was deeply involved in occultism, she was living at her father's home when she met Sidney Webb. Her sister Theresa married Sir Alfred Cripps of the Labor Government of Ramsay McDonald and the third sister, Georgina, married Daniel Meinertzhagen, a banker-affiliate of the East India Company.

Richard Potter was deeply steeped in occult theory and practice and is believed to be the central character in the children's witchcraft novel *Harry Potter* that recently "came out of nowhere" to become a runaway success, but which we now know was one of Richard Potter's tales revamped by the Tavistock Institute and then given to an Joanne K. Rowling to "write."

Many of its goals which I first enumerated in 1991, have since been achieved, or are well on their way to being achieved. Of special interest in the Committee of 300 programs is the core of their economic policy, which is largely based on the teachings of Malthus, the son of an English country parson who was pushed to prominence by the British East India Company (BEIC), upon which the Committee of 300 is modeled).

The Origin of the New World Order: The East India Company and its successor, the British East India Company

The East India Company (EIC) was chartered in 1606 during the fading years of Queen Elizabeth I, the last monarch of the Tudors. Its men were sent to India to establish good relations in the pursuit of trade with the Moguls and princes and their merchants and banker, following in the footsteps of the Venetian Levant Company. It was the patriarch of the power elite, a sort of a "royal family" consisting of the London Staplers guild and its offspring, the London Mercers Company. These "royal family" family trading monopolistic guilds were anchored in Venice and Genoa among the ancient Black Nobility banking families.

In 1661 Charles II of the Stuarts granted the East India Company a far-reaching charter that allowed the EIC to wage war, to engage in peace treaties, to make alliances with the political and mercantile banker-princes of India.

Whether the Mogul Empire broke up because of the East Indiamen's activities is not certain, but it is assumed by historians that they did nothing to prevent the end that came by the year 1700. It would take another 130 years for the EIC to subdue almost the entire Indian subcontinent during the course of which the company there was a falling-out and a split followed by unification when it became known as United East India Company, and later, the British East India Company (BEIC).

One of the most important lessons the East Indiamen learned from the banking-princes was the art of fractional reserve banking as it was to become known in Europe and the United States. It was introduced into England in 1625. The East Indiamen were able to gain access to the inner secrets of banking in India and to send back to London; the fullest details of how the system had worked for centuries in India and how it had been copied by the Babylonians.

Contiguous with the rise of the powerful company were the families of the "300," which included Churchill, Russell, Montague, Bentham, Thomas Papillon and Bedford among them. In the United States it was the Delano, Mellon, Handiside Perkins, Russell and Colin Campbell families who prospered mightily from the EIC and its opium trade carried out with opium from India.

One of the most important members of the East India Company was Jeremy Bentham, "King-maker" of the East India Company. Bentham was the leader of the pre-Fabian *Philosophical Radicals* and was the first person to openly declare in favor of a One World Government. His ideas were formulated into what is now called "utilitarianism philosophy."

Bentham led the British East India Company from 1782. Owen went to the U.S. to found Socialism at New Harmony on the Wabash River. The word "Socialism" as a political creed was apparently used in this way for the first time in 1830.

Robert Owen played an important part in shaping the course of U.S. politics. Together with Francis Wright they toured the U.S. preaching free love, atheism, abolition of slavery (in conjunction with the "Secret Six") and founded what was probably the first Socialist institution, the *Workingman 's Party* in New York City in 1829. It is important for the reader to understand that Owen's mission was to carry out the "300" agenda for the United States:

To establish Socialism as the forerunner of Communism.

> ➤ To destroy the family as a unit by preaching "equal rights" for women and causing division of family members.
> ➤ To establish "boarding schools" the object being to separate children from their parents for lengthy periods of time.
> ➤ To establish 'free love" as an accepted norm with abortion, "to get rid of an inconvenience" when necessary.
> ➤ To establish a movement that would push for the amalgamation of races into a One World population.
> ➤ To secretly and clandestinely establish the Luciferian Society. In later years Professor Arnold Toynbee was to head this most secret society, both in England and the U.S.

Owen hated the U.S. and State Constitutions and worked with John Quincy Adam's son Charles Francis Adams to establish the forerunner of the Federal Interstate Commerce Commission.

In 1808 James Mill met Jeremy Bentham and the two formed a close friendship. In 1811 he became associated with Robert Owen. In 1819 Mills was received into the Secretariat of the East India Company.

The importance of this appointment should not be overlooked. Already, at that time the British East India Company had virtually full control over the entire Indian sub-continent and was paramount in the vastly lucrative opium trade in China using opium from poppies grown in the fertile fields of the Ganges and Benares valley. The profits were staggering, even by today's standards, while the cost of the product was negligible.

Later Mills was promoted to head the Secretariat and was thus in control of a vast empire, political, judicial and financial with huge sums of money to be administered. He had charge of the *"Court of Directors,"* the top men who shaped policies that affected the entire world at that time, including the United States and Russia. His economic theories found favor in many quarters and especially with David Ricardo who formulated the *Theory of Rents* that became standard Marxist doctrine. His son, John Stuart Mill succeeded him as head of the Secretariat, a position of power and influence he held until the British Government took over the political side of the company in which later became officially known as the British East India Company (BEIC).

By 1859 the BEIC reached the height of its immense power by following the policy of John Stuart Mill that if there was to be lasting stability, there had to be absolute power in the hands of wisest. Power and wisdom coincided, the doctrine of the East India Company—and the Philosophical Radicals likewise.

From 1859 the British East India controlled the British government and exerted great influence on world affairs. The United States was its constant concern in that the sheer size and diversity of the country made it difficult to control In fact the BEIC could be observed as having taken control of every aspect of life in the country. Whereas the Philosophical Radicals had been able to carry out much of the agenda of the East India Company, the United States presented a more complex challenge, primarily because of the State and Federal Constitutions.

As I have so often stated, we have been misled into believing that the problem I am talking about began in Moscow when in fact it originated with the radical left, of the Hussites and the Anabaptists, several of their leaders having immigrated to the United States. Americans have been brainwashed into believing that Communism is the greatest danger we are facing. This simply is not so. The greatest danger arises from the mass of traitors in our midst. Our Constitution warns us to be watchful of the enemy within our gates.

These enemies are the servants of the Committee of 300 who occupy high positions within our governmental structure. The *United States* is where we must begin our fight to turn back the tide threatening to engulf us, and where we must meet and defeat these traitors within our national gates. But this is a difficult task. The proponents of a One World Government-New World Order have reduced the American people to a word-conditioned people. The American people have become a nation of conditioned and indoctrinated people who unlike their ancestors are ready and willing to accept "authority."

We have witnessed the rise of the Neo-Bolshevik elements embedded in the Republican Party, supposedly a conservative party. But under the leadership of President George W. Bush, a candidate for the office chosen by the "300," we have seen the United States transformed into a belligerent power attempting to impose the will of the "300" on the world. The Club of Rome created the 25 year-war in El Salvador, as an integral part of the wider plan drawn up by Elliot Abrams of the U.S. State Department.

If only we, in the United States, had statesmen and not politicians managing the country, how different things would be. Instead we have Tavistock agents like Bernard Levin writing Tavistock mind— conditioning material, which is sold as philosophy in Club of Rome publication concerning how to break down the morale of nations and individual leaders.

Here is an extract of one of Levine's articles:

> One of the main techniques for breaking morale through a strategy of terror; consists in exactly this tactic: keep the person hazy as to where he stands and just what he may expect.
>
> In addition, if frequent vacillations between severe disciplinary measures and promise of good treatment, together with the spreading of contradictory news, make the

structure of the situation unclear, then the individual may cease to know whether a particular plan would lead toward, or away from his goal. Under these conditions, even those individuals who have definite goals and are ready to take risks, are paralyzed by the severe inner conflict in regard to what to do.

This Club of Rome blueprint applies to countries as well as to individuals, and in particular, to the government leaders of those countries. We, in the United States need not think, "Oh well, this is America, and those kinds of things just do not happen here." Let me assure you that they *are* happening in the United States—perhaps more so than in any other country.

The manner in which former President Richard Nixon was forced out of office was typical of Levin methodology. Had Nixon not become demoralized and confused, and had he stood his ground, there was no way that he could have been impeached. The Levin—Club of Rome plan is designed to demoralize us all, so that in the end we feel we should follow whatever it is that is planned for us. We will follow Club of Rome orders, like sheep. Any seemingly strong leader, who suddenly appears to "rescue" the nation, must be regarded with the utmost suspicion.

With the U.S. spiritually, and morally bankrupted, our industrial base destroyed, throwing 40 million people out of work, our big cities ghastly cesspools of every imaginable crime, with a murder rate almost three times higher than any other country, with 4 million homeless, corruption in government reaching endemic proportions, who will gainsay that the United States is ready to collapse from within, into the waiting arms of the New Dark Age One World Government?

Could anything be more chilling or dangerously sinister?

Other Club of Rome members in the U.S. were Walter A. Hahn of the Congressional Research Service, Ann Cheatham and Douglas Ross, both senior economists. Ross's task, in his own words, was to "translate Club of Rome perspectives into legislation to help the country get away from the illusion of plenty." Ann Cheatham was the director of an organization called "Congressional Clearing House for the Future."

From time to time the Club of Rome holds gatherings and conferences which because they appear under innocuous titles appear to be of little threat to our country. At these meetings, action committees are formed, and each assigned a specific task and a specific target date by which time their assignments must be brought to a successful conclusion. NAFTA and the World Trade Agreement were two such projects. As I said in 1981, we are set up, politically, socially and economically so that we remain locked into the Club of Rome's plans. Everything is rigged against the American people.

If we are to survive, then we must first break the stranglehold the Committee has on our government. In every election since Calvin Coolidge ran for the White House, the Committee has been able to plant its agents in key positions in government, so that it matters not who gets the White House post.

Proof that the Committee of 300 exists is something I am often called upon to provide.: Walter Rathenau, a prominent Socialist politician and financial adviser to the Rothschilds—and one can imagine how powerful Rathenau must have been, wrote an article in the Wiener Press, which it published on December 24, 1921.

In the article quoted in the *Committee of 300*, Rathenau made this astonishing comment:

> *Only three hundred men, each of whom knows all others, govern the fate of Europe. They select their successors from their own entourage. These men have the means in their hands of putting an end to the form of State which they find unreasonable.*

Exactly six months later, on June 24, 1922, Rathenau was assassinated for his indiscretion. One hundred years ago, this could not have happened, but now it has happened and excites little comment. We have succumbed to long range penetration warfare waged against this nation by Tavistock. Like the German nation, defeated by the Prudential Insurance Bombing Initiative, enough of us have succumbed to make this nation the kind that totalitarian regimes of the past would have only envisaged in their dreams. "Here," they would say, "is a nation, one the largest in the world, that doesn't want the truth. All of our propaganda agencies can be dispensed with. We don't have to struggle to keep the truth from the nation; it has willingly rejected it of its own volition. This nation is a push over."

This is being quite openly proclaimed in world councils and forums as the end of the old era and the beginning of state of being, which is beyond a conspiracy.

It is the world proclaimed by H. G. Wells, what he called *The New Republic*. That New Republic is now beyond the Conspiracy and it is being led by the controllers of the United States especially chosen by the Committee of 300 over whom we have no control.

Chapter 16

War & Paper Money

T he post-war struggle over the redemption of $550 million dollars in Greenbacks, sold for $250 million in gold, is part of the story, but is outside the scope of this inquiry. Thus paper money became the instrument for war, and tyranny regained a foothold on the American continent. The victory of 1776 was turned around.

Returning to Patterson and King William, being an intelligent readership, you are going to ask questions. Patterson, you will say, provided the means to circulate partly backed paper money, but who provided the actual goods needed to wage the war? It is a good question. The answer is—**the very same people who refused to pay for the war by increased direct taxation now provided the goods, through the ruse of paper money,** enabling King William to take their goods by means of subterfuge, one which depreciated the value of their money at the same time. His subjects were not presented with a true bill for the cost of the war; it being hidden from them; but nevertheless they paid the cost of it just the same.

The exact thing happens every time the U.S. goes to war. We are never told how much the war is costing, and because government dare not risk a revolt, the war is financed by indirect taxation; i.e. through paper money; un-backed fiat money, printed in ever— increasing amounts without any backing. The English people were also deprived of their right to debate the issues. This still happens today, especially once propaganda is introduced. During such times, when propaganda takes over, reasoned debate is thrown out and emotions run high. Nearly every school and university in America teaches that America went to war twice in recent years in order to preserve democracy, and because America's liberty was threatened by Germany.

It was never explained how a nation with only 95 million people and demographic limitations, with little in the way of natural resources could hope to achieve its alleged objectives.

Apparently there were not enough people willing to ask the question. America became the victim of skillful propaganda emanating from the "think tanks" of the Royal Institute for International Affairs, and the Tavistock Institute.

Germany was not the aggressor in either World War One or World War Two. Objectionable, treaties were created like the one between Britain and Czechoslovakia to ensure that war would occur.

In the case of America, war was ensured by the Lusitania incident for which Germany was blamed. And in the Second World War it was Pearl Harbor. One wonders that the conspirators were able to get away with such blatant propaganda, but we saw worse things during the Vietnam era, so perhaps it is not too hard to understand how the U.S. succumbed to massive amounts of propaganda, which swept the country into two world wars.

We saw the same thing happen again in Korea and Vietnam; and it is happening again today, in front of our very eyes in Central America, the Balkans, Africa and the Middle East, especially in Iraq. Ever since the Civil War, Rothschild's agents, who were also agents for the Black Nobility, were hard at work trying to establish a Central Bank in the U.S. They did not intend to let a patriot like Andrew Jackson stand in their way. To the public just prior to 1905, this was an arcane issue because it was not understood, and the people did not understand that it would profoundly affect every living soul in America if the Rothschild crowd got their way.

During 1905, J.P. Morgan planned a small depression in the US economy, designed to get the people to clamor for protection against any future depressions by creating a Central Bank, which Morgan said was necessary to protect the "small man" from becoming the victim of depressions. J. P. Morgan, the fiscal agent for several European countries, a fact disclosed by the late great Louis T. McFadden, then set off his planned depression in 1907, and panicked the people into demanding a Central Bank to protect them. Depressions are caused solely for the purpose of transferring unearned wealth from the people who created it, to the aristocracy who did not earn it.

The Aldrich Bill was initially defeated because the public saw Aldrich as being too much in Belmont's pocket. But the bill's sponsors persevered until they succeeded. With the loss of freedom brought about by the new Federal Reserve Bank, the stage was set for an explosion in the supply of paper money, not by fractional reserve or normal business loans; that was too slow, but by the means whereby America could enter the war, which had begun in 1914. Although the public never realized what the bankers were doing, several Congressmen did, and they attacked Morgan and Warburg. Men like Congressmen LaFollette and Lundeen; included Rockefeller in their criticism.

This is found in the *Congressional Record,* Volume 55, pages 365 to 372, of April 5th 1917:

> *By 1917, Morgan had floated huge loans, which he figured would be guaranteed by America's entry into the war within two years. (He was accurate in his calculation). Morgan was surrounded by admirers of the aristocrats and feudal families of Europe and America. One such man was Herbert Crowley, a true lover of medieval aristocracy. Morgan knew the power of the press and he used it as his personal propaganda machine in order to create a hysterical anti-German atmosphere. According to Congressman Calloway, Morgan gained control of the most influential newspapers by buying them with un-backed fiat paper money. He staffed them with*

12 of his hirelings who were more interested in damaging America than in serving it. These influential newspapers then became nothing more than propaganda mills. Reasoned debate fled. Hysteria replaced it; the small peace movement was overwhelmed.

The American Revolution changed all that. It directed the hostility of the people to the correct target, the aristocrats and smashed their grip upon this land. Unfortunately, the same Colonists, or I should say their descendants, did not see as clearly the slavery behind the Federal Reserve matter; to them it was an arcane issue, and so, what was gained in 1776, went by default in 1913. The covert aristocracy, warned of by Jefferson, imposed its yoke of servitude upon the American people with passage into law of the Federal Reserve Act of 1913. The date was no accident; it barely scraped under the wire of their timetable for war, which was declared in 1914. Without the paper money "created" by the Central Bank and there would have been no world war.

Covert aristocracy lives by exploiting the producers of real wealth, the people, and transferring the wealth produced by the workers into themselves by a variety of ruses, thereby in fact, living as parasites off the people. It is really almost the same system that was employed by the open aristocracy of the Dark Ages, when the feudal lords bound the peasants to the land, so that they could rob them of the fruits of their labor, and also take their women forcibly since they saw peasant life as cheap and exploitable, more possessions. The aristocrats of America also regard people's lives as cheap. Have not millions of our men given their lives in fighting two world wars? The only difference is that our feudal lords, the Marshalls, the Harriman, Mellon, Fields, Pratt, Stillman, Aldrich, Rockefeller, Cabot Lodges, Guggenheimer, Kuhn Loeb, Morgan, Warburg, etc. are covert aristocrats, while their European counterparts are open aristocrats. This did not apply to the Soviet Union where the aristocrats who ruled the country were actually covert aristocrats, although they called themselves the Politburo, the Communists, etc.

Open aristocracy is a state publicly declared, while covert aristocracy operates underground, which is the way the greater part of the world is ruled today in 2007.

Genuine democracy does not exist, since the majority of the people throughout the world, including America are not allowed to keep the fruits of their labor. It is withheld from them by a variety of undemocratic methods, and then transferred to the underground or to the open aristocracy.

To be an aristocrat takes great wealth, which must be acquired, since a parasite never ever works. And paper money has proved a boon to this class, since it enables the wealth earned by the people to be transferred to them in a steady manner. When the going gets slow; wars are created to speed up the transfer process. So without any thought for the suffering they caused, the noble lords of America sent millions of Americans to their deaths in both world wars, not only to enrich themselves and entrench their power, but also to get rid of what they considered was an excess number of people.

Had the government of the day been forced to resort to a drastic direct tax-hike to pay for the war, ardor for war would have been dampened at once. But with the mechanism provided by the Federal Reserve, there was no need to announce to the people that they were being led into disaster. Enthusiasm for war was whipped up by well-trained experts from the Royal Institute for International Affairs and Tavistock sent in to do the job. Against such organizations, the populace had no defense. Any national leader like Charles Lindbergh, who saw through the whole dirty trick was immediately neutralized; in the case of Lindbergh—the kidnapping-death of his infant son.

When war hysteria erupts, men lose all reason. Ability to debate issues is lost in a welter of induced patriotism, issues are decided on the basis of emotion, and the principles of freedom and justice are abandoned for the supposed good of the nation.

Patriotic songs, flag waving and martial music takes the place of careful judgment. Were it possible to catch the attention of the population at such a time of induced mass-hysteria for war, then theoretically we could beat the big drum of the hidden cost of the war and strip the covers off of paper money, and point out that power to debase our money for the benefit of the few, rests with the very people who are agitating for war. We could explain that the purpose of the war is to enrich the entrenched aristocrats in their position of absolute power. We might even be able to show that war is not for the good of the nation, and that bankers do not have a monopoly on patriotism.

We might even be able to explain the connection between paper money and wars with huge profits going to the bankers. We could prove that by aggregating the wealth in their hands, the aristocrats are actually the enemies of freedom, not its defenders, and that they are as bad, if not worse than the Communists, because the wealth, which they have aggregated unto themselves, is never capitalized to produce more wealth for the good of the nation. We could certainly prove from this standpoint that the people were being asked to fight a war for the defense of an unchristian principle, that of false capitalism. The correct principle for our Republicanism is Christian capitalism, which has no common ground with Socialism.

My message is quite a change from the hideous cacophony of hissing, cackling and howling, which passes as "news" on the TV screens each night. We, the People, are no longer sovereign because we allowed our Congressional representatives to give away our sovereignty in 1913 to a group of faceless men, who are at enmity with our Republic; men, who regard us as expendable peasants. No wonder Hosea said that we perish for lack of knowledge. Our people didn't know what the Federal Reserve System stood for in 1913, and the majority of us still don't know it now.

It is clear that the victory of the Colonists in 1776 was undone by proliferating vast amounts of partly or totally un-backed paper money, of which there are three types:

> The banker's license to issue more paper than he has gold or some other measure of real wealth with which to back it entirely.
> Where the central banks lend smaller banks gold in time of crisis.
> Legal Tender, which removes the measuring scale of gold, (scales keep people and nations honest) and replaces it with legal tender paper, which is backed by nothing, not even a promise to pay in real money. It isn't money, but government says that we must accept it as such, and lo and behold—we do! If we once stopped accepting paper money, wars would be impossible to start without stiff new taxes.
> The proliferation of paper money occurs because it is not supported a fixed base, such as gold, but on an ever—expanding base of paper money, a veritable daisy chain of paper. Generally speaking, all these methods were used to finance wars in the past and the greater the proliferation of the daisy chain, the longer the wars lasted. Conversely, as soon as a country reverted to gold backed currency or metal currency, altogether, wars wound down rapidly. Specie payment is a great cure for war! No **real** money equals no war without a huge direct tax being levied at the risk of a rebellion.

America was truly free for a while, thanks to the genius of Thomas Jefferson, who saw the world entering into a period of slavery under covert aristocracy. He understood the role of paper money and he understood the intended role of the Central Banks. He knew that bank paper is a license to steal, and a central bank is merely the mechanism whereby that license is issued and grossly expanded. He also knew that un-backed paper money spells slavery.

When you steal from a man, and he is powerless to do anything about,—it that is slavery! Jefferson saw that the proposals of the aristocrats for a central bank were only a rehash of the control exercised by the nobles over the peasants in the Dark Ages.

President Andrew Jackson carried on the bitter struggle to abolish the central bank, which in spite of every obstacle, he succeeded in doing. America entered upon a period of rapid economic expansion, proving how right Jefferson and Jackson were. The American nation had thrown off the yoke of the parasite; they were free to produce as much real wealth as their talents permitted, but more importantly, they were allowed to keep the fruits of their labor. All that changed with enactment of the Federal Reserve System into law. And I want you to remember, the Federal Reserve System started from scratch in 1914 without a single penny, yet by 1939, for example, the system had reaped a profit of $23,141,456,197. Not one single penny of it went to the government of the people, which does not own one single stock in the Bank! (The figures are taken from *Congressional Record*, May 19th 1939, page 8896).

The way had been opened for the aristocrats to steal the fruits of our labor, exactly as they stole the fruits of the peasant's labor in Europe in the Middle-Ages. In World Wars I and II, and American soldiers were packed off to Europe and the Pacific to fight bloody wars to preserve banker's loans and perpetuate the system of slavery imposed by the Federal Reserve Act of 1913.

Jefferson explained that we as a nation faced two enemies; an external one, and the internal one. Both Jefferson and Lincoln said that the internal enemy represented the greater danger to our Republic and our freedom. While America's attention is directed toward the more visible of the two, which today is so-called "Global Terror " the aristocrats grow stronger and even more powerful, until in 2007, it is the covert aristocracy that represents a terrible danger to our continued existence as a nation based on republican ideals of freedom. And the way it was accomplished was through paper money.

It will be recalled that Morgan and his mini-depression of 1907 was followed by the empty slogan, that the small people would never again face bank failures if only the government would consent to a Central Bank? Well, let us look at what happened since then.

The record shows that more banks have failed since a Central Bank was established in this country in 1913, than in any other time in our history! Worse yet, since then we have become bondsmen, because very one of us owes interest, and when we owe interest we are bondsmen, and what is a bondsman, but a slave of course!

What makes servitude possible? Of course, it is paper money!

The Aristocracy's answer is to create bigger budget deficits, which will further proliferate and thus expand the supply of unbacked paper money, so that the few may be further enriched at the expense of the people. When the whistle was blown on the huge cost overruns of the Minuteman missile project, for its failure, the Lockheed Company was awarded a large subsidy by the government, which came just in time to pay its heavy legal bill incurred through the Fitzgerald disclosure.

This is an example of an enemy within. We need not fear the distant enemy as much as the internal enemy. If needs be, the nation can marshal its huge resources in a short time and defeat any external enemy. We demonstrated our ability to do that in World War II; only history will show that we fought the wrong enemy! What then was the true purpose of wars in which the U.S. became embroiled?

Was it to defend against a primitive semi-savage people and their weak culture, people like the Vietnamese for example? No, it was to turn our attention away from the real enemy, the parasites which infest our national body, just as the feudal lords deflected and discharged hostility outward, and away from themselves toward an imaginary danger. The Roman Empire always excited foreign wars to the same end.

Geographically, America is fairly safe from invasion, and we have the technology to defend ourselves against anything any enemy may have. But what happened? The aristocrats acting through their hirelings like Robert McNamara forced us to abandon our best defense against ICBM missiles. Yes, we abandoned our shield.

After stalling for years and arguing against it, McNamara, the hireling of the aristocrats, refused to spend the money appropriated by Congress for our finest particle beam weapons which could be placed in space, from where they would have been capable of blowing up every enemy missile aimed at the U.S. before it reached its intended target!

You would think that there would be a clamor to install such a defense. On the contrary, the same people led by the same McNamara went around the country preaching a chorus of hate against beam weapons! And the news media said the weapons are what it calls "futuristic" as if it were a crime! *Newsweek*, the mouthpiece of the internal enemy, calls beam weapons "Star—Wars"! Let us take another of the hirelings of the aristocracy. Henry Kissinger.

Kissinger left office years ago, but he is still covertly running the country's foreign policy. *Time* magazine reports that he is an influential visitor to the White House. Kissinger says he is a great admirer of Prince Metternich. Since Austrian history isn't exactly a popular subject in our schools of learning, not many Americans know what he stood for. Metternich was the Prime Minister of Austria in the 19th century, a devoted disciple of feudalism. It was against this authoritarian tyrant that President Monroe directed his famous Monroe Doctrine.

Robert McKenzie, in his book, *The 19th Century; A History*, has this to say about Metternich:

> *His (the Emperor Francis of Austria's) theories about government dispensed with not only popular interference, but with popular criticism. He allowed no liberty of thought or speech; he kept his people in abject submission, believing that to be for their good.*
>
> *He enforced a strict censorship over the press, and a vigorous scrutiny of all printed matter, which came from abroad, that foreign agitators should not disturb the happy tranquility, which the absence of thought might be expected to produce. He upheld a minutely ramified system of secret police, by which he would have timely warning if unhappily the contagion of liberalism reached his people.*
>
> *For all his measures for suppressing the intelligence of his people, and preserving untarnished that ignorant loyalty without which he believed government impossible, he was ably supported by his wily and unscrupulous minister. Prince Metternich; A more absolute despotism never existed among men than that which was maintained to the close of the emperor's life.*

Now you know what Kissinger would do with us, if ever he gained absolute power over this country. It was Kissinger derided who spat upon the Monroe Doctrine, and trampled over Monroe's grave with cloven hooves. I am referring to the disgraceful blot upon the pages of our American history, the Malvinas War, when we sided with the Queen of England in her war against Argentina.

We betrayed Jefferson, Jackson, and Monroe. We fouled our own nest by breaking the Treaty of Rio, which we signed and thereby obligated ourselves to repel any and all attackers who ventured into this hemisphere. We showed the world that we are an unreliable ally, one not to be trusted to keep our written obligations,—and we did it again with the Gulf War and the destruction of Serbia! Where did the money come from to pay for these disgraceful adventures? Why, it came from the printing press or fresh air money!

Opposing war is a difficult, lonely and often dangerous business. When war hysteria is being generated, bankers go about loudly proclaiming their patriotism. Any one who doesn't join in the clamor for war is tagged for smearing as "unpatriotic." I do not speak of the small element, who opposes war for the wrong reasons, people who follow Jane Fonda, who used the Vietnam War to promote Socialism; they can be dismissed with the contempt they deserve. I am talking about genuinely patriotic men and women, who will examine the true motive for war, and discover that it is nothing but a way to underwrite banker's loans and enrich the aristocracy.

Of course there have been a few times when war was fought for real freedom, as in the case of the American War of Independence, and the Boer War in South Africa, but they are rarities. The best way to defeat the plans now being laid for the next war is to phase out and dispense with un-backed paper money, and return to a gold denominated currency based on gold at $700 per ounce. Then we must actually balance the budget. In spite of the loud cries from Congressmen from both parties, the bankers haven't the slightest interest in this ever happening. They use their hirelings to make loud noises for a balanced budget, but it is all a bluff and a sham.

Were we to abolish the deficit by balancing the budget, it would result in a big jump in interest rates. The creators of real wealth, we, the people, could no longer be exploited quite so easily, as government could not so often be able to go to the printing press to run off money it needed. Instead, government would have to go to the same market as corporations do in order to borrow the money, and for a time this would send interest rates out of sight. Wall Street would not soon recover from such a thunderclap.

The empty rhetoric used by politicians to garner votes so that they can stay in office would give way to instant action. Great pressure would be applied to government to hurry up and balance the budget so that no more borrowing was necessary. Military inefficiency resulting in waste would be halted. Instead of being vilified, people who stood up to this would be hailed as heroes! We must abide by the Constitution to stop undeclared wars, which are not in our best interests. No more undeclared wars like Korea, Vietnam, Yugoslavia and the Gulf Wars. If we ever have to fight to preserve our freedom and liberty, then government must place the matter squarely before the people without propagandizing it.

We must debate all the issues and decide on what course of action to take, and if it is war, then let it be called war, and not the Gulf of Tonkin Resolution. Now that we are an Empire, let's call our military by its proper name, the Department of War, not the Department of Defense! Moreover at such a time the government must tell the people how the cost of the war is to be met. No more wars via paper money. That must go! No more subterfuges to get us involved in wars to reap profits for the bankers! No more Gulf Wars. Lets us get beyond the conspiracy.

A case in point is when American troops first went uninvited to Vietnam; it was on the excuse that they were going to help in relief work for flood victims. They stayed on, and war was the result. War must be recognized by the definition of Clausewitz: "War is the continuation of politics by other means."

Vietnam was entered into by stealth and deception on a grand scale without a formal declaration of war. Kissinger prolonged it when it was thought it might end too soon. Kissinger kept the Paris "peace" negotiations dragging on and on,—all the while placing the blame for the delay on the Vietnamese.

This enabled the bankers to make the game worth the candle in the way of profits. That delay killed more of our men in the meat—grinder; it did not seem to matter.

Wars reap huge profits for the bankers. Rothschild made $4 billion dollars out of the Civil War. Nobody knows how much was made out of the two World Wars, Korea and Vietnam. What is certain is that the next war is being planned right now (does the government, otherwise why talk about the draft?) But it will not be a nuclear war. The bankers on either side have no intention of destroying each other's assets. In the two World Wars, there was an unwritten agreement not to bomb munitions factories for the same reason.

The next war will be another half-and-half-meat-grinder war. If you have doubts about it, look at what is already taking place in the Middle East. If the U.S. needs to be involved in the Middle East, then the President must show the people of this country exactly on what legal grounds we are to go to war. He must also tell us what it will cost, and how we are to pay for it. Then Congress must declare war, and send our forces to war there with the object of winning the war in the shortest possible time.

There is a proven link between paper money in all wars since 1694. Take the period 1915 to 1917, in which we saw a huge increase in the supply of paper money coupled with a dramatic fall in its purchasing power. War is not arranged for the common good, with notable exception of the war in 1776, but for the benefit of those who draft the legislation and reap the profits, and if the great benefits which flow to the aristocrats from paper money financed wars were to be cut off, there would suddenly be little reason for going to war, in fact it would become unpopular.

Andrew Jackson took on the Black Nobility, the bankers of Europe and America, and he defeated them. He stood foursquare on the Constitution and he overturned their moneychanger's tables, as Christ did before him. He was not afraid of the Supreme Court.

When Justice Marshall handed down an unconstitutional verdict, Jackson said: *"Marshall has made his decision, now let him enforce it."* Jackson recognized that the Supreme Court is not above the Constitution, and that We, the People, are the only ones who can enforce the Constitution. Later, Marshall seeing the error of his ruling came to the same conclusion. Without paper money America would not have entered either World War. We had no reason to get involved.

The Senate said so. After a careful investigation into the cause of the First World War, it issued document 346 and I quote from it:

> *Their responsibility rests solely upon the shoulders of the international bankers. It is upon their heads that the blood of millions of dying rest.*

Some 12 million people perished in that war. The Nye Committee and the Sisson Committee found no good reason why we should have sent our army to Europe in 1917. The English were never known as an aggressive or war-like nation until the use of un- backed paper money was established by the Bank of England. Then England fought one war after another and became the "gamecock" of Europe, as the following list indicates:

1689–1697 King William's War

> ➤ 1702–1713 Queen Anne's War
> ➤ 1739–1742 War of Jenkins' Ear
> ➤ 1744–1748 King George's War
> ➤ 1754–1763 French and Indian War
> ➤ 1775–1783 American Revolution
> ➤ 1793–1801 War against Revolutionary France
> ➤ 1803–1815Napoleonic Wars

The only war which England did not win was the American Revolution, and it will perhaps give an insight as to why the aristocrats were so shocked at losing to the American colonist, after such a long string of successes.

England was at war for 126 years from 1689 to 1815, and while it is true that she was not on the battlefield all of this time, we can consider it as being at war, since the intervening years when the army was not on some battlefield, it was getting ready to go to war.

Similarly, America was not an aggressive nation until paper money took hold, then we went to war twice, and fought in two wars, that we had no rhyme or reason to become involved in. We twice attacked Germany without provocation.

The Senate's *Nye Report* published in 1934 stated that America had absolutely no reason to go to war in 1917. Since then, David Rockefeller ensured that no such report would be issued concerning the Second World War and United States involvement in it. In a CFR document, which Rockefeller commissioned immediately after the close of hostilities in 1945, it was stated that the CFR did not want to see any discussion about the reasons for going to war for the second time in Europe, such as followed the First World War. He commissioned a 3-volume history of World War II to silence historians who might seek to expose what really happened. There is only one method in which the aristocrats can get nations to go to war for them again, and that is through the use of un-backed fiat currency, such as we have in the Federal Reserve notes that pass for "dollars" and which I have endeavored to show you, is an instrument of tyranny. We must redouble our efforts to regain the freedom brought to this continent by the American in 1776.

We do not enjoy freedom today in 2007. As watchmen of the walls, we must do what we can to enlighten our fellow countrymen, so that our bondsmen status is brought home to as many of them as possible. If necessary, then we must not hesitate to reawaken the spirit of 1776. It is our constitutional right to force changes in government when we, the people are not satisfied. America is the last bastion of freedom, but our freedom is rapidly being whittled away by the internal enemies and if We, the People think that America is worth saving, then we have both a right and a duty to take the necessary action to correct what we do not like. Don't send your sons and daughters to another war made possible by paper money! Let us resolve to get beyond this great conspiracy by exposing it far and wide for the gigantic fraud it really is.

Other titles

OMNIA VERITAS. OMNIA VERITAS LTD PRESENTS:

JOHN COLEMAN

ABORTION
GENOCIDE IN AMERICA

BY JOHN COLEMAN

ABORTION
GENOCIDE IN AMERICA

I MAINTAIN THAT WHEN A WOMAN AGREES TO
AN ABORTION IN A NON-LIFE THREATENING
SITUATION, SHE HAS TAKEN LEAVE OF HER
SENSES AND SHOULD BE ADJUDGED
"TEMPORARILY INSANE."

ABORTION SHOULD BE EXPLAINED AS EUPHEMISM FOR "MURDER BY DECEPTION"

OMNIA VERITAS. OMNIA VERITAS LTD PRESENTS:

JOHN COLEMAN

The many tragic and explosive
events of the 20th century
didn't happen by themselves,
but were planned according to
a well-established pattern...

THE CLUB OF ROME
THE THINK TANK OF THE NEW WORLD ORDER

BY JOHN COLEMAN

THE CLUB OF ROME

Who were the planners and creators of these major events?

OMNIA VERITAS. OMNIA VERITAS LTD PRESENTS:

JOHN COLEMAN

DIPLOMACY BY DECEPTION
AN ACCOUNT OF THE TREASONOUS CONDUCT
BY THE GOVERNMENTS OF BRITAIN AND THE UNITED STATES

BY
JOHN COLEMAN

DIPLOMACY BY DECEPTION

The story of the creation of the United Nations is a classic case of diplomacy by deception

OMNIA VERITAS LTD PRESENTS:

DRUG WAR against AMERICA

The drug trade cannot be eradicated because its directors will not allow the world's most lucrative market to be taken away from them...

BY JOHN COLEMAN

The real promoters of this cursed trade are the "elites" of this world.

OMNIA VERITAS LTD PRESENTS:

FREEMASONRY from A to Z

by John Coleman

In the 21st century, Freemasonry has become less a secret society than a "society of secrets".

This book explains what masonry is

OMNIA VERITAS LTD PRESENTS:

THE ROTHSCHILD DYNASTY

by John Coleman

Historical events are often caused by a "hidden hand"...

Who is guilty? Who commits the crime or who denounces it?

This is a trilogy describing the role of the American corporate socialists known as the Wall Street financial elite

Jews have a very particular relationship with money...

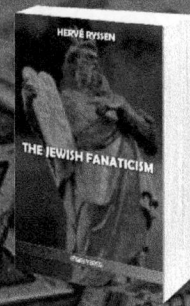

OMNIA VERITAS — Omnia Veritas Ltd presents:

The Jewish Mafia

HERVÉ RYSSEN

The Jewish mafia is, however, undoubtedly the most powerful mafia in the world. The most dangerous, too. Some overly curious journalists have already been killed.

The "Jewish mafia", that one, does not exist; the Western media do not talk about it...

OMNIA VERITAS — Omnia Veritas Ltd presents:

MURDER BY INJECTION

THE STORY OF THE MEDICAL CONSPIRACY AGAINST AMERICA

by EUSTACE MULLINS

The cynicism and malice of these conspirators is something beyond the imagination of most Americans.

OMNIA VERITAS — Omnia Veritas Ltd presents:

NEW HISTORY OF THE JEWS

Throughout the history of civilization, one particular problem of mankind has remained constant.

by EUSTACE MULLINS

Only one people has irritated its host nations in every part of the civilized world

OMNIA VERITAS — Omnia Veritas Ltd presents:

THE BLACK GOLD SPIES

The story of the series of secret agents who, since Napoleon I and the Great Game, precipitated the collapse of the Ottoman Empire and then obtained control of the world's oil supplies

by GILLES MUNIER

THE BLACK GOLD SPIES

This saga is akin to an adventure story

OMNIA VERITAS — Omnia Veritas Ltd presents:

THE CONTROVERSY OF ZION

by Douglas Reed

Douglas Reed's book is the missing link unveiling the multisecular plot.

Zionism: Centuries of Struggle to reclaim the Holy Land

Resurrected true history !

OMNIA VERITAS — Omnia Veritas Ltd presents:

The plot against the Church

by MAURICE PINAY

It can be stated without fear of exaggeration that no book in the present century has been the object of so many commentaries in the world press...

A magnificent and imposing compilation of documents and sources of undeniable importance and authenticity

9 781805 401391